Decorating With Houseplants

Created and designed by
the editorial staff of
ORTHO BOOKS

Project Editor
Marianne Lipanovich

Writers
Larry Hodgson
Dr. Charles C. Powell

Additional Text
Donald M. Vining

Designer
Gary Hespenheide

Ortho Books

Publisher
Richard E. Pile, Jr.

Editorial Director
Christine Jordan

Production Director
Ernie S. Tasaki

Managing Editors
Robert J. Beckstrom
Michael D. Smith
Sally W. Smith

System Manager
Linda M. Bouchard

Editorial Assistants
Joni Christiansen
Sally J. French

Marketing Specialist
Daniel Stage

Sales Manager
Thomas J. Leahy

Distribution Specialist
Barbara F. Steadham

Technical Consultant
J. A. Crozier, Jr., Ph.D.

Address all inquiries to:
Ortho Books
Chevron Chemical Company
Consumer Products Division
Box 5047
San Ramon, CA 94583

Copyright © 1993
Chevron Chemical Company
All rights reserved under international and
Pan-American copyright conventions.

1 2 3 4 5 6 7 8 9
93 94 95 96 97 98

ISBN 0-89721-226-6
Library of Congress Catalog Card
Number 92-71351

Chevron Chemical Company
6001 Bollinger Canyon Road
San Ramon, CA 94583

Acknowledgments

Illustrator
Paul Kratter

Photography Editor
Pamela Peirce

Editorial Coordinator
Cass Dempsey

Copyeditor
David Sweet

Proofreader
Fran Haselsteiner

Indexer
Trisha Feuerstein

Layout by
Cynthia Putnam

Composition by
Laurie A. Steele

Associate Editor
Sara Shopkow

Production by
Studio 165

Separations by
Color Tech Corp.

Lithographed in the USA by
Webcrafters, Inc.

Designers
Carolina West Designs, San Francisco: 81; CoClico & Co. Inc., Interior and Exterior Landscape Design, San Francisco: 26; Cois Pacoe Design, Sausalito, Calif.: 14, 80, 88; Helen Craddick, John Wheatman & Associates Inc., San Francisco: 16, 19; Craig Dinsdale, San Francisco: 98–99; Nancy Doolittle Residential Design, Palo Alto, Calif.: 30–31, 95; Nancy Glenn Design, Sausalito, Calif.: 20, 27, 43; The Kreiss Collection, San Francisco: 82, 89; Gary Millar, Oakland, Calif.: 98–99; Ruth Livingston, Tiburon, Calif.: 12, 13; Mary C. Peck Interiors, Menlo Park, Calif.: 9, 97, 102; Myra Posert, Laura Ashley Interior Design Service, San Francisco: 8; Nan C. Rosenblatt/Gabrielle Whitney, San Francisco: 11; Carlos Sanchez, Sanchez-Ruschmeyer Interior Design, San Francisco: 17, 24; Ruth Soforenko Associates, Palo Alto, Calif.: 4–5, 6, 29, 45, 57, 77, 83, 86, 87, 96; Jonathan Straley, John Wheatman & Associates Inc., San Francisco: 59; Van Fleet Construction, Ashland, Oreg.: 59; John Wheatman, John Wheatman & Associates Inc., San Francisco: 15, 22, 44, 62, 64–65, 78–79, 95.

Special Thanks to
Nathan Bennett
Mr. & Mrs. Jonathan W.B. Crosby
John Demergasso
Geoffrey A. Gatz
Kenneth and Marilyn Lavezzo
Janet Lennox Moyer
Harold and Susan Muller
Marina Ricciardi
Plants Unlimited, San Lorenzo, Calif.
Wes and Laurie Rose
Barbara Waldman, Designer Preview, San Francisco

Photographers
Names of photographers are followed by the page numbers on which their work appears.
R=right, C=center, L=left, T=top, B=bottom.

Bill Apton: 100
M. Baker: 108T
Laurie Black: 8, 11, 12, 13, 14, 16, 19, 20, 22, 26, 27, 43, 80, 81, 82, 88, 89, 108B, back cover bottom left, back cover bottom right
John Blaustein: 54
Clyde Childress: 94
Richard Christman: 38BL
Alan Copeland: 18, 34
Douglas Evans: 103T
David Goldberg: 41, 50, 53T, 53C, 56, 74, 76B, 84, 95T
Saxon Holt: 103B, 109
Michael Lamotte: 58
Michael Landis: 52, 66, 106
Fred Lyon: 39
Michael McKinley: 44, 85
James McNair: 93
Ortho Information Services: 37, 40, 53B, 63, 68, 69, 71, 72, 73, 76T, 76C, 90, 92, 101
Pam Peirce: 49, 51, 104
Karen Stafford Rantzman: Title page
Kenneth Rice: Front cover, 4–5, 6, 7, 9, 10, 15, 17, 23, 24, 29, 30–31, 36, 38TL, 38TR, 38BR, 45, 47, 55, 57, 59, 60, 62, 64–65, 75, 77, 78–79, 83, 86, 87, 95B, 96, 97, 98–99, 102, back cover top left, back cover top right

Photographic Plant Stylists
Milana Hames
JoAnn Masaoka Van Atta

Front Cover
Plants add the finishing decorative touch to any room. In this sunroom, a kentia palm (*Howea forsterana*) and a kumquat (*Fortunella margarita*) frame a comfortable reading chair while a grape-ivy (*Cissus rhombifolia*) drapes softly across the table and around the potted geranium (*Pelargonium*). Flowering lace-cap hydrangeas (*Hydrangea*) brought in from the garden add spots of color.

Title Page
Bromeliads, orchids, palms, and succulents share a living space. Either alone or in combination, choosing just the right indoor plants will add the finishing touch to any decor.

Back Cover
Top left: A bright yellow orchid accents a hallway arrangement of baskets and chest.

Top right: A kitchen window is the ideal growing spot for this indoor herb garden.

Bottom left: Chrysanthemums provide seasonal color in this plant-filled corner.

Bottom right: A shrimp-plant (*Justicia brandegeana*) and miniature primroses (*Primula*) brighten this living-room table.

For a more dramatic effect, the weeping fig can be replaced by its more tolerant cousin, *Ficus maclellandii* 'Alii', whose long, strap-shaped leaves provide the look of the Far East to any interior.

That other office institution, the cornplant (*Dracaena fragrans*), fits well in the home. Three to five individual plants of this trunk-forming species can be placed in a pot to make one full, fan shape. Although palms will not survive in the darker area behind a sofa, a cornplant usually will as long as there's a window nearby. In dark locations a cornplant's growth is extremely slow and overwatering becomes a danger.

Another tall, fan shape is the variegated screwpine (*Pandanus veitchii*). A mature specimen is striking and the same size as a large indoor palm. The whorl of long, tapering blades, which spring from the stem in a perfect spiral, are bordered with yellow and striped along their length with pale green bands. The screwpine can be killed by prolonged exposure to temperatures below 55° F but will survive nearly every other condition. Give it a sunny location and watch it grow.

In southern California and other warm climates, dwarf banana trees (*Musa* species) in tubs can occasionally be brought inside to provide a tall, fan shape. Patio-grown citrus or loquat (*Eriobotrya japonica*) can also be brought inside. These plants can be grown indoors the year around in an especially sunny location.

Other good choices for a tall, fan shape include the spiky, spineless yucca (*Yucca elephantipes*), the spreading umbrella tree (*Brassaia actinophylla*), and the China-doll (*Radermachera sinica*).

Low, Bushy Shapes

Low, bushy plants look handsome sitting alone on the floor next to a low piece of furniture, softening the lines of the furniture by their roundness, or filling any other ground-level design space. They are also particularly effective on stands. In fact, if you place one of these plants on a tall stand (at least 4 feet high), it can substitute in design terms for a tall plant. Low, bushy shapes are best used alone rather than in combination with other plants (plants in this category are too large to be considered as tabletop plants).

A peace-lily (*Spathiphyllum* 'Mauna Loa') has an excellent low, bushy shape, and like the cornplant (*Dracaena fragrans*), it grows well in low light. When it is thriving it sends up white flags (the showy spathe cradling the real flowers), signaling contentment, not surrender.

Philodendrons are also highly suitable low, bushy candidates. The lacy-tree philodendron (*Philodendron selloum*) is popular, although its leaves may flop with age and poor light.

A particularly dependable low, bushy shape is the cast-iron plant (*Aspidistra elatior*). The common name carries a genuine recommendation, for this plant has a hardy constitution that makes it ideal for situations where other plants will suffer. Unlike most of the tropicals, which grow all through the year, aspidistra has a lengthy dormant period during which it is surprisingly undemanding. During dormancy it can be placed anywhere, window or no, and the cooler the room the better. When growth resumes in late winter, it requires good light,

The low, spreading shape of these grape-ivies (Cissus rhombifolia) *does not overpower the small area beneath this window. Plant stands bring the ivies to the desired height; their natural spreading characteristics prevent them from growing too tall for the space.*

water, and fertilizer. Aspidistra benefits from a summer spent either outdoors in deep shade or in a moderately bright, well-ventilated room.

A mature pot of Chinese evergreen (*Aglaonema*), especially of a type such as 'Silver Queen', makes a showy display. This philodendron relative looks like a small dieffenbachia with its gray-green, cream, and emerald leaf patterns, but it is not as coarse as the latter. Chinese evergreen sends up new shoots from the base of mature plants; it soon fills the pot, the many leaves overlapping each other. It, too, is very tolerant of low light.

The Kaffir-lily (*Clivia miniata*), whether in flower or not, is a good decorative choice even though it won't survive in dim light. Use a pot that is large enough to hold several individual plants so that there will be several bloom spikes (one per plant). Kaffir-lily spends most of the year in a bloomless state, but its black-green, straplike leaves are extremely decorative. When the plant is in bloom, it is resplendent with clusters of yellow-throated, orange trumpets, 10 to 15 on each spike. It requires a cool, bright, dry dormancy in late fall and early winter; then, in late February or early March,

This dramatic Pachypodium *punctuates the decor like an exclamation point, creating a focus around which the rest of the room is decorated. The spreading orchid cactus* (Epiphyllum) *behind the couch is a counterpoint to the* Pachypodium's *strong vertical line.*

when the flower spikes appear, it needs warmth, light, water, and fertilizer. During summer Kaffir-lily can be grown outdoors in deep shade or in bright, indirect light inside.

Orchids (*Cymbidium* species) are also low, bushy plants. In some varieties both the straplike leaves and the flower stalks arch. Orchids do best in a cool greenhouse, but while in bloom they can take a turn indoors. The uncut blooms last for six to eight weeks.

Column Shapes

Sometimes space restrictions dictate a column shape—an exclamation point of a plant that stands like a sentinel. A column makes a more formal architectural impression than does the tall, fan shape. Generally speaking, the sparer and more hard-edged the decor (a minimalist or high-tech interior, for example), the more appropriate a columnar plant becomes.

Giant cacti and succulents, barely distinguishable from contemporary sculpture, are obvious examples. Many euphorbias are very sculptural in appearance, often looking like branching baseball bats. Peruvian apple (*Cereus peruvianus*) has a similarly sculptural appearance.

Other naturally columnar plants include the coarse-leaved ficus plants, including the familiar rubber plant (*Ficus elastica*). (It should probably be renamed the supermarket ficus, since it's so often sold there.) Although the species is all green, several of its cultivars have greater color interest and will grow in an upright column unless forced to branch by pruning. This is also true of the fiddleleaf fig (*Ficus lyrata*), which deserves more popularity.

Many plants that do not normally grow as columns can be trained into upright forms through the use of cedar slabs, stakes, or poles covered with sphagnum moss and wire that serve as posts for plants to cling to as they grow. Among them are the large-leaved Red Emerald philodendron, Algerian ivy (*Hedera canariensis* 'Variegata'), kangaroo vine (*Cissus antarctica*), grape-ivy (*Cissus rhombifolia* 'Ellen Danica'), and the arrowhead vine (*Syngonium podophyllum*).

Soft, Feathery Shapes

Airiness can be a desirable characteristic in decorative plants, making them appear soft, refined, and gentle—a green cloud rather than a thunderbolt. Airiness can soften a hard-edged interior or complement a busy, heavily patterned, ultradecorated room.

The weeping fig (*Ficus benjamina*) is the ultimate airy tree, which accounts for much of its popularity in interior decorating. Another popular feathery tree is the Ming aralia (*Polyscias fruticosa*). The Ming aralia is also the most fickle of trees, full of leaves one moment, denuded the next, and requiring absolute consistency in care and location.

Podocarpus is also worth investigating. This weeping plant has a long, needlelike leaf and an arching habit. It makes an elegant columnar plant, although it may require permanent staking to keep it upright. A south window and life on the dry side improve its growth.

Among the smaller feathery plants, asparagus fern (*Asparagus densiflorus* 'Sprengeri') is a popular choice. This common plant drapes itself over anything in its path, turning hard objects into soft, shapely forms. An upright plant with feathery leaves is the false-aralia (*Dizygotheca elegantissima*). If overwatered, however, it will rapidly lose its leaves.

Softly draped curtains, a light, floral-patterned slipcover, and a spring bouquet are complemented by the feathery plumes of a fern pine (Podocarpus gracilior).

Strong, Graphic Shapes

Sometimes a background will cry out for a plant with a bold pattern or form that will serve as a focal point, especially against a solid wall of color. Line—not mass—is what is required. In this situation, the Madagascar dragontree (*Dracaena marginata*) is a good choice, especially a mature specimen with many trunks. The spiky umbrella of foliage cascades from the ends of the branches, and the interplay of the beige trunks below makes a beautiful display. Many growers deliberately train the trunks into contorted, angular shapes when the plants are young to achieve a striking, graphic effect.

The ponytail-palm (*Beaucarnea recurvata*), with its furrowed bark and elephantine base, also has a strong sculptural presence, as do mature, multiple-trunk specimens of *Yucca elephantipes*. In addition, many succulents have strong lines, but they require sunny locations.

Graphic shapes are generally large and strong, as this bird-of-paradise (Strelitzia) *demonstrates. The plain clay container, smooth floor, and simple lines of the settee show the plant to its best advantage.*

Flowering Plants

Except for an occasional oleander (*Nerium oleander*) or Chinese hibiscus (*Hibiscus rosa sinensis*), flowering houseplants seldom achieve sufficient size to make a design statement; in other words, they rarely look most effective standing alone. Flowering plants are best used as tabletop decorations or as centerpieces among foliage plants.

View blooming houseplants as long-lived bouquets. For the price of cut flowers, you can buy a great deal of living color that will last much longer. Instead of a bunch of daisies, for instance, you can buy a pot of cineraria (*Senecio × hybridus*). Any quick list of flowering houseplants is rich in variety: kalanchoe, begonia, azalea, guzmania, florist's gloxinia (*Sinningia speciosa*), African violet (*Saintpaulia*), Cape primrose (*Streptocarpus*), primrose (*Primula*), cyclamen, star-of-Bethlehem (*Campanula*), ornamental pepper (*Capsicum*), hydrangea, amaryllis (*Hippeastrum*), heather (*Erica*), pocketbook-flower (*Calceolaria crenatiflora*), sapphire-flower (*Browallia*), flamingo-flower (*Anthurium*). You may have other favorites. Some of these are available only seasonally, but many can be bought the year around.

Although flowering plants are an easy way to add a dash of color, you can't expect them to perform continuously. Cut flowers don't last forever, and neither do flowering plants. You should set them in their plant stations (see below), enjoy them, and then either discard them when their blossoms fade or return them to an out-of-the-way growing station, making space for plants that have just come into bloom.

If you need a more dramatic effect than one or two small plants can give, place several (alike or different) together in a bowl, tray, or basket. You can also add some newly purchased plants to your current display for a more lavish look. (In horticultural circles, adding new plants to a display is known as refreshing your garden.)

ESTABLISHING PLANT STATIONS

To design effectively with houseplants, start by deciding where you'd like to locate plants without regard to light or other practical considerations. Would you like to see a plant arching out from behind a favorite table and chair combination or at the end of the sofa to soften a

Top: The perfect plant station and just the right plant for it can be found for even the sparest of rooms. This bold, out-of-the-ordinary set of blooming amaryllis (Hippeastrum) arranged in a basket with Scotch broom (Cytisus scoparius) and Spanish moss (Tillandsia usneoides) complements this sleek and unadorned kitchen.
Bottom: With its bright blooms and long-lasting colored bracts, this living-vaseplant (Aechmea fasciata) introduces subtle color to a room.

hard edge? Would you like to flank a doorway with a matched pair of plants to create a sense of formality? Perhaps you've always wanted to put a small plant on a desk or a bookshelf or in the middle of the dining table. The places that seem to call for a plant, places where a plant is a perfect decorative statement, are called plant stations.

A plant doesn't have to be at its station all the time, and the station doesn't have to be occupied by the same plant all the time. The ficus tree by the window can be moved into a dark corner on special occasions and lit from below for drama. Two specimens of the same kind of plant can be alternated weekly between a dark station and a brighter one. For instance, you might rotate two philodendrons between a bright bedroom window where a large plant is needed and a spot in the curve of the grand piano where there is no light at all. If you have a sunny window, a light garden (see page 44), or a greenhouse, you can prepare plants for display and return them when their moment on the stage is over; then the understudies (another set of plants) fill their roles.

How welcoming to walk into a windowless entrance hall and be greeted with a display of bulbs in bloom. Your guests won't know that if they had visited the week before the bulbs would have been in hiding and their station occupied by aspidistras. Restocking plant stations in this fashion keeps the displays fresh. The coffee table in the living room can be graced by a small plant that's been on a bright windowsill or under fluorescent lights elsewhere in the house. It can be changed from week to week according to what is blooming. Essentially, you can be your own florist.

What would be the plant stations for a corner of a room furnished with a wing chair and a round pedestal table? An obvious one is on the table, but that may not be the best design solution. The spaces that need filling are around the grouping of furniture, behind and above the table and chair or on each side of them. There are at least three good architectural solutions: a low, fan-shaped plant on the floor beside the table; a tall plant in the corner behind the table and chair; or a combination of both, with a third plant on the floor on the other side of the chair for balance. There are no rules for plant placement, only ways of thinking about how plants can fill space and relate to other shapes in the room.

Another common situation is a long buffet against the dining room wall, with a chair at either end and a large bowl in the middle. Where are the plant stations? The voids are on both sides of the bowl. The chairs fill the voids at the ends of the buffet, and the bowl fills the middle. A pair of candlesticks or two vases of flowers could fill the empty areas between, but a pair of plants would lend the same formality to the setting in an unusual manner. A plant could replace the bowl, or the bowl could be moved to one side and balanced with a plant on the other side. If there is space beyond the chairs, plants could be added there at floor level as a finishing touch.

Obviously, the more elaborate your facilities for growing, maintaining, and rejuvenating plants, the more display stations you can have and the more frequently you can change the plants. Few people remember that potted plants are not fastened in place; it's easy to move them around. Usually, the plant that starts on the windowsill stays on the windowsill and never graces the dining table. Similarly, the African violet (*Saintpaulia*) that's relegated to the coffee table never gets moved to the windowsill, even if it doesn't bloom.

SOLVING DESIGN PROBLEMS

Striking foliage and flowers make useful, relatively inexpensive design tools. They create divisions within a room, add color, alter the scale, fill empty spaces, and obscure architectural defects. A plant can be found to fill almost any design need.

Plants as Room Dividers

Many homes feature large, open interiors. Although you may enjoy the sense of spaciousness, undoubtedly there are times when you wish you had the divisions and privacy that walls and partitions afford. With an effective arrangement of plants you can achieve separation without ruining the open atmosphere.

Mass several medium or large plants, such as croton (*Codiaeum variegatum*), coffee plant (*Coffea arabica*), podocarpus, or schefflera (*Brassaia*). Or perhaps a freestanding weeping fig tree (*Ficus benjamina*) or palm will be enough to block the view and divide the area. Hanging baskets can also divide space—suspend two or three from strong ceiling hooks and fill them with columneas, grape-ivies (*Cissus rhombifolia*), or spiderplants (*Chlorophytum*).

Fragrant blooming paper-whites (Narcissus) brighten this dark corner.

A planter box at a right angle to the front door will help create an entrance area in a small house or apartment where the front door opens right into the living room. A two-sided bookcase makes an attractive and functional room divider with plants interspersed with books and other items on the shelves.

Plants to Fill Empty and Dark Spaces

How many times have you looked around the house wondering how you could make empty and dull corners, blank walls, and unused areas disappear, or better yet, transform them into attractive features? Plants are a relatively easy and inexpensive solution. These spots are perfect havens for shade-tolerant plants, such as palms, dracaenas, sansevierias, scheffleras (*Brassaia*), monsteras, or philodendrons. (Supplementary artificial light will noticeably enhance their performance.) Enliven a stairway with trailing plants set in wall brackets or pots lined along the stairs. Use the pools of space often found around furniture arrangements as a station for several plants.

Plants as Camouflage

Plants can disguise architectural obstructions, converting them into striking design features. For instance, when faced with a bothersome pillar or post in a room, instead of trying to ignore it, use plants to soften its lines and make

The stark firebox in this unused fireplace is softened and filled by the grape-ivy (Cissus rhombifolia).

The bonsai pine
(Pinus) *on the coffee
table and the Japanese
maple* (Acer palmatum)
*temporarily stationed
by the window add
dramatic focal points
without clashing with
the spare decor of this
living room.*

it blend into the room. Encircle the base with a mass of plants or train vines to grow all around it. A warm, sunny corner can be the perfect place to grow plants that prefer dry, warm conditions, such as cacti and succulents. An empty fireplace becomes a perfect growing spot for a Boston fern (*Nephrolepis exaltata*) or a cast-iron plant (*Aspidistra elatior*), providing the chimney is closed to prevent drafts. Protruding angles or recessed areas can be softened and disguised with ferns, piggyback plants (*Tolmiea menziesii*), creeping-charlie (*Pilea nummulariifolia*), and Swedish ivy (*Plectranthus australis*) hung at various levels to create visual interest.

INCORPORATING PLANTS INTO YOUR INTERIOR DESIGN

Interior designs and decorating styles vary almost as much as the many thousands of different plants we bring indoors. In a room a handful

of basic design elements—wall coverings, furniture, ornamental decorations, and the layout—combine to create the style of the room, whether it's Asian, Mediterranean, provincial, Early American, Victorian, or modern. To help plants advance the theme, consider how they blend with the predominant elements in the settings you have selected.

Matching Plants to Decorating Styles

The right plant just seems to belong in a room. Linear, unpatterned modern interiors become warm and comfortable with healthy green plants in their midst. Graceful palms and weeping fig trees (*Ficus benjamina*), with their striking branches, vibrant greenery, and exotic leaf shapes, inject the atmosphere with a natural vitality and calmness unachievable by the architectural decorating scheme alone.

Traditional interiors, such as many Early American and Victorian homes, look attractive

Houseplants are available in a variety of sizes and shapes to match any room. These two weeping figs (Ficus benjamina) are in perfect proportion to the dimensions of this hallway.

with displays of ferns or palms, which fit in well with ornately carved antiques. A room furnished with provincial pieces takes on an even more antique flavor with the complement of ferns placed on wooden stands.

Southwestern interiors, with their natural colorings, tile flooring, and large windows, are suitable for many plants. Bromeliads, cacti, and succulents—with their striking texture, color, and form—are the most fitting. The more refined Mediterranean interiors will benefit from the stark stems and bursts of pointed foliage of the dracaena, which mixes well with the color and form of patterned upholstery and terrazzo flooring.

Matching Plants to Room Size

Choosing an appropriate size and scale for a plant display is a key factor in making it an attractive focal point within an interior. A plant display of the wrong size or scale can be either visually overbearing or lost.

Small rooms usually look best with a few small plants. You might want to hang a wandering-Jew (*Tradescantia* or *Zebrina* species) in an alcove, grow a mature jade plant (*Crassula argentea*) in a floor basket, and place a podocarpus in a corner. These plants won't cramp the limited space, and their flowing branches may provide a visual relief from the compactness of the room.

For a subtle touch of color, try growing a Cape primrose (*Streptocarpus*), florist's gloxinia (*Sinningia speciosa*), or African violet (*Saintpaulia*) on a windowsill, dresser, or coffee table. Some larger plants to grow in small rooms include bamboo palms (*Chamaedorea erumpens*) and false-aralias (*Dizygotheca elegantissima*). These plants are delicate and subtle. They do not branch widely, but rather grow vertically, consuming little of the precious living space.

Large rooms are far more suitable for the big plants, such as weeping figs (*Ficus benjamina*), monsteras, palms, and large orchids, and for group displays of small and medium-sized plants.

Small plants displayed alone tend to be lost in the spaciousness of a large room, unless they form a theme—the same kind of plant in variations of color or form, for example. Small and medium-sized plants will be more noticeable in large rooms when displayed in similar decorative containers, such as placing them all in brass or ceramic pots.

Displaying Plants

The presentation of plants can make the difference between decor and mere clutter. Decorating with African violets (*Saintpaulia*), for instance, is no easy job. The plants are small, and avid growers often have dozens of them covering every available surface or crowded into fluorescent light gardens. The crowding detracts from their appeal. Individually, the plants are quite beautiful, but not necessarily noticeable, particularly in an unimaginative green plastic pot. To be decorative they must be properly presented.

One way to show off a single small plant is to place it, pot and all, into a small cachepot (the French term meaning *hiding pot*) or decorative container that matches or complements the bloom. Set the cachepot on a round, black stand just slightly larger in diameter than the cachepot. Immediately, the unassuming plant becomes a star.

Two important display principles are illustrated here. First, the mechanics must not show. The green plastic pot with the rolled edge that African violet growers prefer is part of the mechanics. It is serviceable but not

The exquisite blue-and-white china cachepot and dark plant stand spotlight the jewellike beauty of this African violet (Saintpaulia)

attractive. The decorative cachepot makes the presentation work. And if it has no hole in the bottom like most cachepots, it has the added advantage of keeping water from dripping on the table.

Second, whatever you want to display must look important. Isolate a single plant from its fellows, spotlight it, put it in a showy pot, and set it on a stand. Any accessory looks more important when it is placed on a base. The stand and the cachepot can then be placed wherever they look best, and the spot becomes a new plant station. The violets can be rotated between the growing area and the display station.

Plants that are dressed up and viewed one at a time are often more enjoyable than those customary group arrangements in which some are flowering and some aren't. One special pot will look more attractive than a group of plastic pots set on top of plastic saucers, the complete antithesis of tasteful display.

Choosing Containers

Pots can be as fascinating as the plants they contain. There are bonsai pots, antique American redware pots, handmade clay flowerpots from Italy, dimestore-variety clay flowerpots, colorful glazed pots with built-in saucers, and a large assortment of decorative cachepots that serve as covers for utility pots.

In the Japanese philosophy of plant display, the pot must not call attention to itself, unless that's specifically what you have in mind. Among bonsai enthusiasts, commenting on the pot before you say anything about the tree is a polite way of saying that the tree isn't worthy of attention. Although we may enjoy compliments on our unusual pot choices, strong-colored and garishly decorated containers should be avoided so that the beauty of the plant is always shown to its best advantage.

Be aware that there may be a difference between the best pot size for horticultural

The shallow, oblong container is a natural-looking base for the sculptural shape of the bonsai birch tree (Betula). On the mantle, a matching glazed clay pot provides a neutral setting for the blooming iris.

reasons and the best size for an aesthetic balance. From a horticultural standpoint, it's generally better to use pots that are on the small side. People often repot small plants into large pots, motivated by the generous but anthropomorphic notion that the roots need a big, comfortable pot with room to grow. In fact, what roots need is air, and a giant pot full of wet soil frustrates that need.

If you need a large pot for aesthetic reasons but not for horticultural ones, consider placing the growing container inside a cachepot. When deciding on the size of a cachepot, bear in mind that plants display to advantage when the display pot is not overwhelming. The plant itself should always be larger than its pot. Jade plants (*Crassula argentea*), which have notoriously small root systems, are too often potted in immense containers that overwhelm the plant.

Perhaps the ideal pot from an aesthetic standpoint is a very deep one. Again, use this pot as a cachepot, elevating the growing container inside the cachepot by placing it on a brick or even another pot turned upside down.

Always remember that a special plant should have a special pot. A large, mature, and exquisitely groomed specimen deserves the loveliest pot you can afford. Although the primitive, folksy beauty of redware pots might best set off small ivies, a green antique oriental pot is more suitable for a full-grown sago palm (*Cycas revoluta*). Similarly, although a patterned pot may enhance greenery, it can clash with a flowering plant. The basic principle is to make sure that the pot enhances what it contains.

Cornering Plants

Within the home, furniture arrangement is becoming less formal. Seating pieces are being moved away from the walls: The sofa can be set in the middle of the room facing the fireplace or on the diagonal of the room, at an angle to the fireplace and either at an angle to or facing other pieces of furniture in the room. Or, if perpendicular to a wall, it can face another sofa or a pair of chairs. The contemporary conversational grouping is a return to the Victorian fashion of having a central table with chairs distributed around it at varying distances.

In both the contemporary and the Victorian arrangements, walls are used to display pictures and artwork and are a background for secretaries, breakfronts, armoires, and bookcases. This

Opposite: The lady palm (Rhapsis excelsa) *and peace-lily* (Spathiphyllum) *are permanent residents of this corner. The chrysanthemums provide seasonal color.*

arrangement leaves the spaces between the walls and the seating areas, especially the corners, open for plants.

If one of the corner walls includes a sliding glass door or large window, plants will receive enough light to grow well, in addition to contributing to the decor. If, however, the corner is a dark one, what can be done? One solution is to rotate plants from the corner to a growing area in a lighter part of the house. Another solution is to use grow lights in track lighting that will illuminate the dark corner.

You can also try the mirror trick. A mirrored, freestanding screen or long mirror panels mounted directly onto the wall can brighten a dim corner. When the mirrors are positioned opposite windows, light is reflected into the foliage of the plant, which may be just the boost that a permanent plant needs (although it will have to be a shade-loving species). The decorative bonus is that the mirror image doubles or triples the plant form, amplifying and magnifying even small plants and making them appear much more important.

Elevating Plants

The indoor gardener who wants to decorate with plants would be wise to accumulate a collection of plant stands and pedestals, as well as plant pots and cachepots. Among the most striking low stands are the oriental footed stands used under Imari bowls and Japanese flower arrangements. These black or brown, wooden stands may have elaborate carving. These stands create instant decorating magic.

Any plant that can be hung can also be set on a stand, often to greater advantage. If height is the goal and there is no skylight, pedestals and tall plant stands are an effective alternative to hanging baskets and free the windows of obstructions. They can also add visual impact to the room.

Instead of trying to grow a ficus where a ficus can't grow, use a peace-lily (*Spathiphyllum*) or some other low-light plant on a pedestal to give the height and grace of a tree, in addition to being easier to maintain. Tall stands can also be topped with seasonal displays of forced blooms. In spring, use tulips (10 bulbs per 10-inch pot); in summer, fill the stands with white geraniums (*Pelargonium*); and at Christmastime, display pink poinsettias (*Euphorbia pulcherrima*).

Tall stands and pedestals of different heights act as "trunks," elevating pots of pothos (Epipremnum aureum) to small-tree status. The mirrored walls double, and sometimes triple, the effect.

Hanging Plants

One of the reasons hanging plants are so popular is that hanging them gets them up high. If light comes from directly overhead, the plants thrive; hanging plants flourish best under a skylight. In fact, some exceptionally beautiful gardens combining hanging plants with floor plants and planter boxes have been created around skylights.

Despite their popularity, hanging plants should be used indoors with discretion. When a plant is hung at a window, light floods in from one side, leaving half the plant shaded. The top, which needs the most light, receives the least; it's the tips that are bathed in sunlight. Soon the plant turns leggy, stringy, and unattractive, especially when silhouetted against the window. One solution is to use swiveling ceiling hooks and rotate the plant so that it receives light on all sides, allowing for even growth.

In some situations, however, a permanent window obstruction may be just what's required. Many urban gardeners use hanging plants instead of window treatments to obstruct an objectionable view without completely blocking the light. Others hang plants because there is insufficient space for them elsewhere in the

room or, in the case of herbs, to have them readily available in the kitchen. In these situations, no matter what the species, the hanging plant must be rigorously groomed and turned to prevent spindly, unbalanced growth.

Hanging plants are magnificent in greenhouses, solariums, and greenhouse rooms. There, hanging plants can be thought of as trees without trunks and placed accordingly, not hanging above other things but tucked behind them. A group of several plants, preferably the same variety, hanging together at different levels is a striking way to fill and soften a corner in a glassed-in space. Keep in mind, however, that hanging plants are less attractive hung high overhead, so that it is mostly the base of the pot that shows, or hung from a rod like a line of clothes put out to dry.

Setting a Stage

Staging, a common practice in flower shows, is another way to elevate plants. Usually it consists of placing a plant on an empty, upturned flowerpot to give it a little extra height and raise it above its companions. A second, smaller plant is then set in front of the staged plant to hide its base. Staging can, of course, be quite elaborate, especially when building lush, tall banks of plants.

At home proper staging can turn a motley group of undistinguished houseplants into a showy display. At least one common problem can be easily solved with staging. Many houseplants lose their bottom leaves, either as part of their normal growth pattern or because they have dried out once too often. To hide a defoliated stem on a tall plant, stage a companion plant (or two plants at different levels) in front of it, and then disguise the staging with a third plant (or more, if necessary) at windowsill or floor level. This pyramidal grouping will amplify the visual impact and be more attractive than any of the three plants alone.

People who are credited with having an eye for designing with plants often have simply learned to stage well and to fill in the front of a plant display so that there are no visible gaps. If the display is raised, a trailing plant should be added in front. An ivy or any cascading plant whose leaves hang over the edge of the container will break and soften the hard lines of the arrangement, as well as cover up the pots and spaces.

USING COLOR

The major decorative elements of a flowering houseplant are its color, size, shape, and texture. Plants are often chosen to complement the colors and mood of an entire room or of decorative items such as paintings, floor coverings, pillows, or sculpture. For a constant presence of flower color, it is important to plan for a succession of blooms throughout the year, and it is often desirable to change the types of plants to achieve this effect. To keep a display colorful, you need to become familiar with many types of plants.

The primary objective in decorating with flowering houseplants is to introduce colors into the room. Color is a basic element of design because it is so easily perceived. Furthermore, colors carry familiar connotations of mood and spirit. Some colors are hot and exciting, others are brash and unsettling, and still others are cool and smooth. A brief review of some of the attributes of color will help you select the appropriate indoor flowering plants.

Shades of green will always be a part of the visual effect of even a flowering houseplant. Greens generally promote a soothing, restful mood. Green will unify and pull together yellows and blues, isolate and call attention to reds and oranges.

Although white is a neutral decorating color, the whites of blooming houseplants are commonly shades of cream, with accents of yellow,

This staghorn fern (Platycerium bifurcatum) flourishes under a skylight, benefiting from the even light it receives. The peace-lily (Spathiphyllum), grape-ivy (Cissus rhombifolia), Boston fern (Nephrolepis exaltata 'Bostoniensis'), maidenhair fern (Adiantum), and weeping fig (Ficus benjamina) lining the tub also appreciate the overhead light.

Deciphering a Plant Name

Family, genus, species, variety—the world of plant names can be confusing to the beginning gardener. But once you learn what these words refer to, plant names are no longer a mystery. And since many plants have the same common name, only by using the botanical name can you guarantee that the plant you want is the one you get.

Plants are classified by division, class, order, family, genus, species, subspecies, variety, and cultivar. For the home gardener, however, the important classifications are genus, species, and cultivar.

Genus refers to a group of plants within a broad plant family that are closely related horticulturally. In a botanical name, the genus is listed first.

Each genus is divided into species. This is the second part of the botanical name. Subspecies and cultivar are often used interchangeably to refer to plants that differ slightly from the species, for example, in flower or foliage color. A third name listed in italic type is a variety; a name listed in single quotes is a cultivar. Read through the chapters in this book and you'll quickly spot examples of genera, species, and cultivars.

Opposite: Flowering and foliage plants have been carefully chosen and placed to advantage in this garden-inspired living room.

pink, or light blue. White blooms are most striking in large quantities, as in a blooming Easter lily (*Lilium longiflorum*). In groups of flowering houseplants, white improves contrast and creates highlights, brightening any room.

Yellow also brightens almost any room. It is full of life and spirit and is especially welcome on indoor plants in spring. Yellow can lighten the heaviness of large blue or purple objects and will accent and complement any blue or green surfaces.

Orange is a mixture of yellow and red, and carries some of the feelings of both those colors. Orange accents earth tones, and in small amounts will intensify or set apart the coolness of blue.

Red is a strong, hot color, usually used in moderation. Orange-reds are commonly used to blend or pick out highlight colors from fabrics or room accessories.

Pink is somewhere between red and blue. Hot pink has the same effect as red; bluish pinks are cool and formal. Pink is a softer color than red and can be used with reds to tone down their effect. Pink flowers convey a warm, friendly mood.

Purple and lavender, like pink, fall between red and blue. Whereas pure reds are rather demanding, shades of purple are cooler and more formal. Lavender is softer than purple. Both colors tend to recede and are sometimes lost in a room, but they can be brought out if combined with white.

Most blue flowers are actually shades of violet or blue-green. Thus some blues appear warm and some cool. Plants with blue blossoms can be blended with greens to create a spacious feeling. Try using houseplants with blue flowers where a stronger-colored flower might overwhelm the setting.

DESIGNING INDOOR GARDENS

Large, architectural plants and the flowering beauties that temporarily fill plant stations operate as loners for the most part—they are striking specimens that make a design statement on their own. Yet most indoor gardeners don't garden with a few striking plants. If you have more than four potted plants, you probably have a great many, and if they are competing for light and attention, they probably look more like a hodgepodge than a garden. However, collections of potted plants, small and large, can make interesting, well-ordered indoor gardens.

The Skylight Garden

Many people who have skylights don't realize that they have an opportunity for a superb garden. This is the best situation for hanging plants, since all the light is coming from overhead. Many flowering plants as well as foliage plants are well suited for skylight gardens.

Hang plants around the sides of the skylight, some high and some low. If there is nothing directly under the skylight, such as a table or passageway, this striking cascade of plants could reach to the floor. You might like to build a large pebble tray of the same size as the skylight and create a floor-level garden to mirror the one hanging above. Attaching a metal grid just beneath the skylight also lets you hang plants directly beneath the opening, where they will benefit from the even light.

Designing a hanging garden around a single plant variety can create a spectacular effect. A display of six columneas will draw more praise than a random view of assorted plants. Try using several varieties of the same plant, creating a little variation in color and form. Choose plants that renew themselves from the center. They will maintain their beauty longer and have a more luxurious appearance than vining plants, with their ever-lengthening stems.

The spiderplant (which was originally called the airplane-plant because of its flying offsets) is especially luxurious looking. The all-green variety, *Chlorophytum comosum,* is a stronger grower than the variegated variety. Ferns of all kinds, especially the Boston ferns (*Nephrolepis exaltata* cultivars), and fernlike plants such as the popular asparagus fern (*Asparagus densiflorus* 'Sprengeri'), renew themselves frequently from the center.

Pots of trailing plants can be kept full, high, and bushy in the center by introducing small rooted cuttings of the parent plant into the same pot. Hanging pots, by the way, should be plastic. Clay pots are very heavy, and their natural porosity allows the potting mix to dry out too quickly.

The Windowsill Garden

An unplanned assortment of plants sitting on a windowsill does not make a garden. More often than not, it makes a mess. However, plants can be successfully arranged around a window. In the late 1960s and early 1970s, sills overflowed with plants that cascaded to the floor, and the glass was covered with plants hanging from ingeniously knotted cords. Today, the window garden has become a less overwhelming affair.

The first rule for a genuine sill garden is that all the pots should match. They don't have to be exact clones, but they should all be clay or all be green, for example. This uniformity focuses attention away from the pots and onto the plants.

Think of the plants as a frame for the window rather than as a screen. Tall plants, such as a snakeplant (*Sansevieria trifasciata* 'Laurentii') or an airy false-aralia (*Dizygotheca elegantissima*), go at the edges or on one side. Medium-sized plants come next and then small plants, so that the arrangement slopes down to the center of the sill. Especially suitable are flowering plants and plants with variegated leaves such as begonias, cyclamens, kalanchoes,

This cheerful indoor garden of flowers and foliage would brighten any room. The dracaena frames one side of an indoor window box filled with bromeliads, heart-leaf philodendron (Philodendron scandens oxycardium), *and asparagus ferns* (Asparagus densiflorus 'Sprengeri').

florist's gloxinias (*Sinningia speciosa*), columnar bromeliads (*Vriesea splendens*), or the beautifully marked Moses-in-the-cradle or oyster plant (*Rhoeo spathacea*). Finally, something should cascade below the sill—a creeping fig (*Ficus pumila*) or a wandering-Jew (*Tradescantia* or *Zebrina* species), for example. If you want a hanging plant, don't suspend it in the middle of the window; substitute it for one of the tall side plants. If the window is heavily draped on both sides, or if you want a more formal look, place one elegant flowering plant in the middle of the sill in an attractive pot or cachepot and omit the collection.

Windowsills can be filled with a rotating collection of houseplants that spend most of their time elsewhere. If the plants are permanent residents, however, choose only those that will flourish on the sill. Remember that window plants must be turned regularly to prevent them from bending toward the light.

Deep bay windows can accommodate many plants without appearing overcrowded. To emphasize the feeling of a garden, consider a pebble tray with sides that are high enough to conceal the containers. The overall effect will be further enhanced if the tray matches the shape of the sill. If the bay extends from floor to ceiling, shape the tray to match the shape of the floor area defined by the bay. For the healthiest plants, provide artificial lighting on the side facing away from the window or turn the plants regularly.

If the plants are growing too close to the glass, damage and poor health may result from cold drafts or the burning rays of the sun. Filter summer sun with translucent curtains, or choose a window shaded by trees in summer. Also, be aware that in summer the high angle of the sun and the shade from the trees can drastically reduce light that was strong in winter and spring. In autumn the window will again get more hours of direct sunlight, as the trees lose their leaves and as the sun sinks to a lower angle, but autumn sunlight is less intense and often obscured by clouds.

The Tray Garden

A group of plants placed together in a container forms a tray garden. The container can be a tin tray with a layer of pebbles at the bottom or a deep planter that hides the pots.

Tall palms anchor a row of matching ferns in this well-designed indoor garden. Daylilies (Hemerocallis) add seasonal color.

In small trays that hold three to five potted plants, repetition is desirable. Three ferns, three syngoniums, three chrysanthemums, or three Reiger begonias make a much better group than a mixture of three different plants. If you do want a mixture, center a tall plant at the back as the focal point, flank it with shorter plants on both sides (still at the rear of the tray), fill in the front with two matching plants, and complete the ends with a pair of plants that cascade and conceal pots, edges, and foliage. This makes a total of seven plants. If a plant is not tall enough to fill its niche, stage it on an upturned pot or saucer. The result will be a plant pyramid.

A variegated plant with plenty of white can be a "spotlight" in a tray garden. Use only one, placed low in front so that it draws attention to itself and to the taller plants behind it.

In a large tray garden, such as an indoor raised bed or planter box, many of the same principles apply. There must be tall plants for focus, but you could also add nonliving sculpture or even fountains. An effective arrangement would include a tall and airy umbrella plant (*Cyperus alternifolius*), a weeping fig (*Ficus benjamina*), or a Madagascar dragontree (*Dracaena marginata*) supplemented with shorter, blooming plants, such as kalanchoes, begonias, azaleas, chrysanthemums, hydrangeas, geraniums (*Pelargonium*), or forced bulbs. This is a good place for seasonal or occasional plants, which you can buy in bloom and then discard or move to an out-of-the-way growing station.

Alternatively, since variegation can substitute for bloom, in the second tier of plants you might use colorful crotons (*Codiaeum*), dieffenbachias, peacock-plants (*Calathea*), or peperomias. Fill in the edges with spiderplants (*Chlorophytum*), grape-ivies (*Cissus rhombifolia*), English ivies (*Hedera helix* and its cultivars), or any ferns. When you've finished, no pots should show and there should be no gaps in the foliage.

The ultimate in tray gardens is a raised bed on casters in which the leakproof tray is deep enough to hide the largest pot and the casters are concealed. The exterior finish can coordinate with or complement the color scheme of the room, and the tray can be moved about the room so that the plants are displayed to their optimum advantage.

The Centerpiece

The center of a dining or occasional table can be one of the most important places to make a design statement. You can emphasize a look that your furniture or color scheme already suggests, or you can create a mood for an occasion with an appropriate, individualized display. If you think of a centerpiece as a design opportunity rather than as a plant, you will realize that any number of plant arrangements can be placed on a table.

An arrangement of jade plants forms an unusual centerpiece that is hard to equal for beauty and durability. Plant approximately one hundred jade cuttings in a perlite and sand mixture in a shallow bonsai pot. When the cuttings have rooted, set the pot outdoors or in an airy, bright room. The little forest can be brought in and placed on the table at any time. Another striking centerpiece can be made from a beautiful blooming plant, such as the Cape primrose (*Streptocarpus* 'Constant Nymph'), set in a deep bowl. Isolate and elevate the bowl on a pedestal and the centerpiece will look especially rich and elegant for the dining table.

The same bowl, this time containing an assortment of apples, oranges, tangerines, avocados, and bananas, is the basis for yet another centerpiece. Make pockets among the fruit, and tuck in small African violets (*Saintpaulia*) or any other small blooming plant. Hide the pots among the fruit and spread the leaves to cover the pockets.

Give your plants as much thought as you would a menu. For a formal dinner, design an arrangement of flowering plants in colors that match or complement the china or linen. For a special party, consider individual plants at each setting. Disguise the containers by wrapping them in napkins that match or set off the ones for your guests. With imagination, your plants will become a complementary part of any table setting.

It is not enough to purchase a plant and set it beside a window. To make a plant feel at home and make a home feel as if the plant belongs, you need to deal with all the design principles that have been described in this chapter. To ensure that plants are healthy at the stations you have chosen (and that you have chosen the right plants), read the following chapters.

Opposite: A moss basket filled with ivy, ferns, and star-of-Bethlehem (Campanula) *makes a charming centerpiece in a cheerful breakfast nook.*

The Basics of Plant Care

Though houseplants may vary greatly in size, shape, and preferred growing environment, mastering their basic care requirements is the basis of any indoor gardener's success.

Houseplants are domesticated wild plants. Over the years, naturally occurring plants have been cultivated and bred to thrive in an indoor environment. The selected plants have one essential feature in common with their wild cousins—adaptability. They can endure filtered light, widely varying temperatures, and the low humidity found in most offices, stores, and homes.

Today, you can select from a wide choice of houseplants, from familiar favorites to the countless new hybrids specifically fitted to the modern interior. Whatever your tastes, choose plants not only for their shape and appeal but also with an eye to where you will place them and how much care they will require.

To make your choice easier, the following pages describe the basic growing requirements of houseplants. You will find discussions on watering and watering methods, growing media, pots and planting methods, preferred lighting conditions for specific plants, and lots more. All of this will help you choose plants to fit your decorating and horticultural needs, and ensure that they remain healthy and good looking.

Healthy plants, such as this maidenhair fern (Adiantum) *and Boston fern* (Nephrolepis exaltata 'Bostoniensis'), *are an essential ingredient when decorating with houseplants.*

UNDERSTANDING HOUSEPLANT BASICS

For the beginning indoor gardener, caring for houseplants can be difficult at first. Watering, lighting, fertilizing, grooming, propagating, and seasonal care are initially bewildering; but they become easy and natural once you understand the basic processes of how plants grow and flourish.

The Parts of a Plant

There are four parts to most plants: roots, stems, leaves, and flowers. All are crucial to plant growth and health.

Roots anchor the plant and absorb the water and minerals that nourish it. Most absorption occurs through the root tips and the tiny hairs on young roots. These tender tissues are easily injured. Transplanting often destroys them, causing the top of the plant to wilt; but under the proper conditions, new root tips will grow within a few days. Roots send water and nutrients to the stem, to start their journey to other parts of the plant. Roots of some plants also store food.

The stem carries water, minerals, and manufactured food to the leaves, the buds, and the flowers. It also physically supports the plant. Stems can store food during a plant's dormant period, and those of some plants also manufacture food. In many houseplants, stems are herbaceous, or soft, rather than woody, as with most trees and shrubs. Whatever their form, all stems function in a similar manner.

The leaf manufactures food for the plant through photosynthesis, absorbing light over its thin surface area. Its pores absorb and diffuse gases and water vapor during photosynthesis, respiration, and transpiration.

The flower is the sexual reproductive organ of the plant. Most plants flower in their natural environment, but only certain plants will bloom indoors. Flowering houseplants are described in further detail in the fourth chapter.

Photosynthesis: Storing Energy

Like all other living things, plants need food for energy. The basic food element for all living things is sugar or other carbohydrates. Unlike animals, however, plants harness the energy of the sun to manufacture their own sugar, through the process of photosynthesis.

In photosynthesis, light energy, carbon dioxide, and water interact with the green plant pigment chlorophyll to produce plant sugars and oxygen, which is released into the atmosphere. The carbon dioxide is drawn in from the atmosphere by the leaves, and the water is provided by the roots. Plant photosynthesis supplies most of the oxygen on our planet.

Photosynthesis requires an environment with adequate light, warmth, and humidity. No amount of fertilizer can compensate for an unfavorable environment, since fertilizer provides only nutritional building materials, not the real food—the sugar the plant manufactures by photosynthesis.

Respiration: Supplying Energy

In plant respiration the sugar created by photosynthesis combines with oxygen to release energy. This energy is used for growth and survival and enables the plant to convert the building materials provided by nutrients found in the soil into plant tissues. Respiration produces carbon dioxide, water, and a small amount of heat as by-products, which are released into the atmosphere.

Transpiration

Sunlight falling on a leaf can heat it well above the temperature of the surrounding air. Transpiration, the movement of water vapor from a leaf into the atmosphere, is important in stabilizing leaf temperatures (keeping them cool), in much the same way that human perspiration has a cooling effect.

As water vapor leaves the plant through leaf pores (stomata), the leaf cools. The higher the temperature and the lower the humidity, the faster a plant transpires. If it loses more water than it can absorb through the roots, it wilts; that is why correct watering is so essential to the survival of a houseplant.

SELECTING PLANTS

Selecting the right plant for a successful indoor garden involves more than simply choosing the first plant that catches your eye. Starting with the healthiest plants possible is one key to success, but wise beginners will also ask for help in choosing plants that suit their homes and their life-styles. Avoid starting out with such difficult plants as orchids or weeping figs

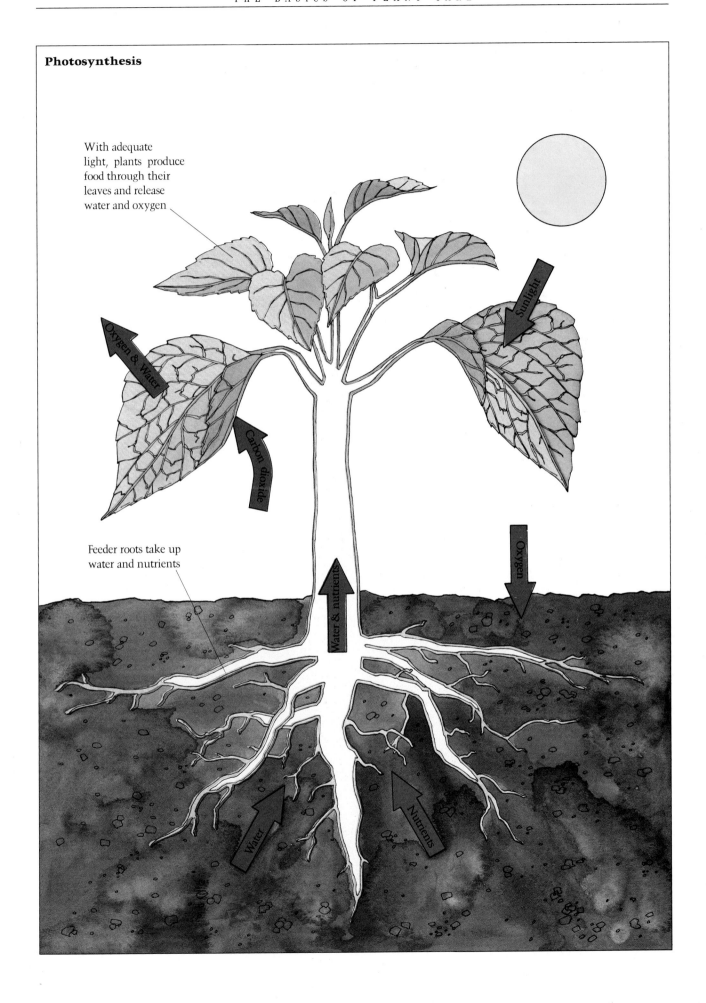

Photosynthesis

With adequate light, plants produce food through their leaves and release water and oxygen

Oxygen & Water

Carbon dioxide

Sunlight

Oxygen

Feeder roots take up water and nutrients

Water & nutrients

Water

Nutrients

Before buying a plant, inspect it carefully to be sure it is healthy.

(*Ficus benjamina*). It is far better to begin with something less touchy and to progress, as skills improve, to more demanding species.

Florida, California, and (to a lesser degree) Texas are the major foliage plant production areas in the United States. Plants of all types and in all stages of development, from cuttings to 20-foot specimens, are available from multi-acre greenhouses and vast growing fields. Depending on the size and type of the foliage and the buyers' specifications, some are shipped directly from the field while others are placed in shade houses to prepare them for the lower light levels they will soon encounter. In both cases, they are boxed and carefully loaded into trucks for shipment to florists, nurseries, and garden centers across North America.

Once delivered, the plants are readied for immediate sale, repotted into larger containers for further growth, or placed under still lower light for more conditioning, or for acclimatization.

Shopping for plants from a truck parked at a gas station or supermarket is risky business. Plants sold this way have most likely not been acclimatized, and their growing and shipping conditions have probably been far from ideal. They are much less likely to survive than plants purchased from a reputable nursery or florist. But often, if plants don't survive, the owners feel responsible. Their feelings of guilt about not being able to keep their plants alive may cause them to give up plant growing instead of just shopping more carefully for replacements that will thrive.

Wherever you shop, be prepared to answer questions posed by a conscientious florist or plant dealer and to ask your own questions. The following checklists will help you find a suitable plant to fit your needs.

Study Light Levels

The most important variable in plant care is light. Will the plant be living in a garden room with skylights? Or, as is more often the case, will it fill a corner far from any light source? The light level (low, moderate, or high) should dictate the plant choice (see pages 40 to 43 for more information on plant light needs).

Compare Plant Needs and Personal Schedules

Some plants require little care; others require a great deal. Some can withstand erratic treatment, such as overwatering one week and neglect the next; others demand systematic, regularly scheduled care. Decide how much care you will be able to give your plants and choose accordingly.

Consider Room Size and Furniture Scale

Buying a small plant and hoping it will grow to fill a particular location is likely to be a frustrating experience; likewise, having to prune a large specimen continually can be very time-consuming and unrewarding. The corner of a room is not a greenhouse, and greenhouse growing conditions can't be simulated in most living spaces. A 2-foot plant is not likely to grow into the 6- or 7-foot tree that the scale of the room demands. And even if it does, will it grow into a graceful or symmetrical plant that suits its setting? It is better to buy a plant that will fit your needs immediately. An added advantage of mature plants is that they generally adapt more quickly to a new environment.

Examine All the Plants on Display

All plants in the display should be healthy. Pick the healthiest plants you can find, and look them over carefully. Plants should have few brown-edged leaves and few or no leaves that have been trimmed, particularly on new growth. They should be full and bushy, with small spaces between the leaves. Large gaps between new leaves suggest that the plant has been overfertilized and crowded to induce rapid growth or that it has spent a long period under inadequate light.

Inspect the leaves and the junctures of stem and leaves for any sign of insects or disease. Insects or diseases brought into the home on a new plant may infect every other plant in your collection. Avoid plants with algae or slime on the growing medium or the pot. Leaves should be free from dust and grime, but should not look unnaturally shiny.

Flowering plants should have many buds that are just beginning to open. Plants in full bloom may already have exhausted much of their beauty. Buying budded specimens is particularly important with those plants that will never bloom again under less than ideal conditions or plants that will be discarded after the flowers fade. If you wish to get the plant to bloom again, refer to the fourth chapter, "Flowering Houseplants."

Check to be sure that the plant fits comfortably in its container. If the roots are showing through the drainage hole, the plant is pot bound; it is best to choose another plant. Flowering plants should be properly wrapped or sleeved at the nursery or florist to protect them during transportation from the store to their new home. Be sure to remove the covering once you get home.

Plants received as birthday or anniversary gifts usually arrive decked out in foil, bows, and ribbons. These decorations may be suitable for the occasion but rarely do they look like an integral part of the decorating scheme of a room. Once the celebration is over, remove the bows and ribbons, and replace the foil with a decorative cachepot or a basket of a shape and size that is appropriate for both the plant and the room.

Consider Plant Costs

Several factors, besides the obvious ones such as rarity and availability, affect the price of a plant. Obviously, if a plant is rare, it will cost more than a plant that is easy to obtain.

The major factor that affects price is the cost that goes into developing the plant before purchase. Species vary enormously in how long it takes or how easy it is to grow them. A kentia palm (*Howea forsterana*), for instance, takes twice as long to reach 5 feet as a parlor palm (*Chamaedorea elegans*); and because it needs

twice the labor and energy to grow to 5 feet, the kentia palm costs more.

Some plants are hardier than others and may be grown in open fields rather than under more expensive greenhouse conditions, so they cost less than greenhouse plants. Two seemingly identical plants of the same species may vary in cost because one was shipped directly from the field for immediate sale while the other was shade grown or held for a period to acclimate it to lower light levels.

ACCLIMATIZING PLANTS

Plants need to adjust to new surroundings; they may even go through a mild case of shock when first brought home. Over a short period of time, the plant has traveled from the meticulously controlled environment of the commercial greenhouse to a different environment at the retailer's and finally to a home with yet another set of light, humidity, and temperature conditions.

Acclimatization takes several weeks. At first, leaves may yellow and blossoms drop. Pay special attention to plant care during this time. A plant that normally tolerates dim lighting may have been grown under strong light and will need time to adjust to the change. Ease the plant through the transition by placing it in interim locations with decreasing light intensity for periods of several weeks or more before placing it in its final site. Hobbyists, especially, will want to isolate new plants for at least four weeks to prevent unnoticed pests or diseases from affecting their collections.

Keep plants moderately moist during this adjustment period; never allow them to dry out. Water thoroughly each time and discard excess water from the drainage saucer. Once a plant is acclimatized to its permanent surroundings, try not to move it too often.

CHOOSING THE RIGHT TOOLS

A few simple tools can make your indoor gardening easier: A long-spouted watering can, good pruning shears, sharp knives, a small trowel, clean cloths, soft sponges, an ostrich feather duster (for small-leaved plants), and soft hairbrushes or paintbrushes are the basic tools the indoor gardener needs. A watering can with a long spout helps you water hard-to-reach plants. Pruning shears and sharp knives ensure clean cuts, lessening the risks of disease and scarring. A trowel helps when transplanting; cloths, sponges, duster, and brushes help keep leaves free of dust and grime; and you'll find a soft paintbrush useful when you are hand-pollinating plants. Most of these items are available at garden centers, hardware stores, and home supply stores.

Most garden centers also stock inexpensive light meters. Light meters indicate whether the light in a particular spot is low, moderate, or high. The readings are not scientifically exact, but they are accurate enough to enable you to choose a suitable plant for a plant station.

Moisture meters are similarly helpful. They don't measure actual moisture; instead, they measure the presence of electrolytes or fertilizer salts in the soil. Since water carries the electrolytes, a high reading ordinarily indicates the presence of moisture. After a while, however, as salts build up in the soil, the meter will give less accurate readings.

Spraying a plant with a mister temporarily increases the humidity around it. More important, misting washes grime from the leaves, and it helps to control pests as well as make plants look healthy and cared for. Other tools that are popular with home gardeners are plastic wrap for layering plants, plastic labels for labeling plants, and a watering wand and a squeeze bottle for watering hanging plants.

You may find you need several sizes of pots, bags of potting soil, plastic flats for rooting cuttings, and powdered rooting hormone. A spray bottle for applying pesticide is also a handy

The right tools make plant maintenance easier. Indoor gardeners will find watering cans and bottles, trowels, scissors, shears, pruning tools, and a mister all useful.

piece of equipment. Be sure to label any pesticide spray bottles and don't store them until they are empty and clean.

WATERING PLANTS

Houseplants are container plants; their roots are confined to the container and cannot reach far for sustenance. Although watering sounds like an easy part of plant care, poor watering is responsible for killing more houseplants than anything else.

Contrary to popular opinion, overwatering is more often the culprit for a plant's water problems than underwatering is. Since the roots can't absorb more water than the plant needs, excess water, unless it drains away, will displace oxygen from the soil. This suffocates the roots and leads to rot. To avoid an overwatering problem, don't assume that a plant needs more water when it doesn't grow as expected; there may be some other reason. Also, never allow a pot to stand in drained water. After watering, pour out any excess in the saucer or remove it with a turkey baster.

Experienced indoor gardeners never water by the calendar. A plant that needs water every day during a hot spell or in a warm room may need it only every other day in cool, cloudy weather or a cooler spot. The amount of water a plant needs varies with the species and its native habitat; the soil in which it is growing; and the light, temperature, and humidity in your home. Plants with a lot of leaf surface or soft, lush foliage will be thirstier than those with less foliage or waxy or leathery leaves.

Water needs are also affected by the growth cycle of the plant. A plant absorbs more water during active growth periods than during rest periods. The size and the type of container are other important factors: In a small pot, moisture is absorbed quickly; too large a pot retains too much water. A plant in a porous clay pot needs water more frequently than one in a plastic or glazed pot. Also, water will run through a pot-bound plant without wetting the roots thoroughly. If you can't keep a plant moist, even when you are watering it every day, it needs a larger pot. Remember: Light, frequent watering is not what most plants need; it is better to water less often and more deeply.

Evaporation also robs a plant of moisture. Some gardeners solve the evaporation problem by placing one pot inside another and insulating

Left: A severely dried-out plant, such as this coleus (Coleus × hybridus), *should be immersed in a pail of water as soon as possible.*
Right: Leave the plant in water until the soil is well moistened or until the bubbles stop. Drain and return the plant to its growing station.

the space between them with peat moss, perlite, charcoal, or gravel. If you do this, be careful not to overwater or the insulation will become soaked. Another way to solve the evaporation problem with small pots is to group them in a wooden box, placing ground bark or peat moss around the pots for insulation and as a temperature-moderating mulch.

The simplest way to find out when your plant needs water is to test by touch. Poke your finger into the soil to feel the degree of moisture. To double-check, rub a little soil between your thumb and index finger; the soil should feel dry to the touch to an inch below the surface, but not powdery. With a little experience you'll be able to tell when the plant needs water. You can also use moisture meters, but the final determination should be how dry the soil feels and how a plant looks.

A plant that is wilting or drooping is thirsty—it needs water at once! Water a plant in this condition thoroughly, and try not to let this happen often—a plant that wilts again and again will not survive long.

Water Temperature

Plants prefer tepid water; cold water can harm roots or foliage, and excessively hot water can kill a plant instantly. Let water from the cold water tap warm up to room temperature overnight. This will also allow the dissolved chemicals present in tap water to evaporate.

After a short time the plant will return to its original healthy-looking state. Do not let plants dry out often because they will not survive this kind of treatment for long.

Water Quality

In parts of the country where the water is particularly hard, it is difficult to grow acid-loving plants, such as camellias and azaleas. However, adding acid soil amendments, such as peat moss, and using acidic fertilizers will help.

Alkaline conditions make it difficult for plants to absorb iron and other trace elements. Regular applications of iron chelate, available at most nurseries, will help to keep the foliage green. When the new foliage on acid-loving plants is yellow, the plant may need extra iron chelate. Water every two weeks with a solution of 1 ounce of iron sulfate in 2 gallons of water until the growth regains its normal color.

Softened water contains sodium that may accumulate in the soil and harm plants. If your home has a water softener, use an outdoor tap for plant water, or install a tap in the water line before it enters the softener so that you'll have a source of unsoftened water for plants. If this is not possible, draw water just before the softener cycle, when the sodium is at the lowest level.

How to Water

Watering plants in the morning allows any moisture on the foliage to evaporate by evening; foliage that remains cool and wet is more prone to disease. Always water thoroughly, until the soil is saturated. If your plant receives only superficial waterings, its roots will grow toward the surface of the soil.

The water should take only a minute or so to drain. If it takes more than 10 or 15 minutes,

Top left: Plants can be watered from above or below. It is usually easier and faster to water container plants from above.
Top right: Plants such as African violets (Saintpaulia) *and other gesneriads are susceptible to water spots when splashed with cold water. Water these plants from below to avoid leaf-spotting.*
Bottom right: Whether watering from above or below, make sure that you water thoroughly and that you pour off any excess drainage water within an hour.
Bottom left: If the plant is too heavy to lift, or if you do not want to remove it from its plant station, use a turkey baster to remove any excess water from the drainage saucer.

the drainage hole may be blocked. Unblock it by poking a stick into the hole to loosen compacted soil. Don't let plants sit in water; if the plant is in a saucer, pour off any drained water within an hour. If the plant is too heavy to lift, use a turkey baster to remove the water.

When water drains through the pot rapidly, it may be running down between the rootball and the pot and not soaking in. This may happen after a plant has been allowed to dry out; it can be remedied by submerging the plant in water to its rim.

Many plants benefit from an occasional thorough soaking; it's the frequency that varies. Check on the watering needs for an individual plant with a houseplant specialist.

Special Watering Techniques

There are times when your plants need more than a shower from a watering can. The following techniques are useful for these occasions.

Submerging   Submerging a pot in water to its rim is excellent for plants that have dried out, plants in full bloom, and moisture-loving plants. Submerging is also the best way to water hanging plants. Place the plant in a sink or tub and leave it submerged for several minutes, until the air bubbles have stopped. Give plants a good soaking approximately once a month.

Showering   An occasional trip to the shower is an effective way to water plants thoroughly and to rinse dust and dirt from the leaves. Use tepid water, with a gentle flow so that the soil does not wash out of the container. Make sure the leaves are dry before returning the plant to direct sunlight, or they may burn.

Leaching   Thorough watering will help wash out accumulated salts, which build up from high salt levels in tap water or from over-fertilizing and can harm the plant. A whitish deposit on the outside of a clay pot or on the inside of the pot at the soil surface indicates salt buildup. Symptoms of salt damage include brown and brittle leaf tips and margins. To leach out salts, place the plant in a sink, tub, or pail and water it several times, letting the water drain each time. You may need to repeat this process weekly for several weeks. Although salt on the outside of the pot will not

harm the plant, cleaning it off will make the pot look better and make it easier to tell if salts are building up again.

Watering terrariums   Once established, closed terrariums need water only once every month or two. Excess water is difficult to get rid of because there is so little evaporation. The best way to tell when a terrarium needs water is by looking at the container itself. When there is no condensation on the glass, and the plants are beginning to droop, add a little water. If this results in extreme fogging (a sign of overwatering), remove the top until the excess moisture evaporates.

Self-watering systems   If you're going to be away for a few days and can't find someone to take care of your plants, you can easily set up a

Many plants, such as this umbrella tree (Brassaia actinophylla), appreciate an occasional trip to the shower to clean the leaves and thoroughly soak the soil. Be sure to use tepid water and a gentle flow so that you don't wash the soil out of the container.

This arrowhead vine
(Syngonium
podophyllum) *is a
victim of phototropism,
or the natural
tendency of plants to
grow toward the light
source. Rotate plants
that lean toward the
light so their growth
will be more even.*

self-watering system. Simply pad a sink or bathtub with matting or any thick, absorbent material. Set pots with drainage holes directly on the matting and moisten the matting. The plants will draw up the moisture.

Here's another temporary self-watering method: Make a wick of nylon stocking or clothesline and put it into one of two small holes in the lid of a plastic refrigerator bowl. Run the wick from the hole in the lid to the drainage hole in the plant container. Fill the bowl with water and cover it with the lid. Make sure that the wick is stuffed well inside the drainage hole and is in contact with the soil. Water will soak slowly from bowl to plant. Commercial wick waterers are also available at many garden centers. For information on self-watering containers, see pages 59 and 60.

LIGHTING PLANTS

For a plant, light means life. Light regulates three major plant processes: photosynthesis, phototropism, and photoperiodism.

Photosynthesis is the method by which plants transform light energy into food energy, as discussed earlier.

Phototropism is the natural tendency of plants to grow toward the light source. The process is controlled by auxins (growth hormones) in the stem tips and youngest leaves. Highly reactive to light, these auxins cause the plant to adjust itself to the light source.

Indoors, where the natural light source is usually a window, plants will bend toward the window. To encourage a balanced shape, rotate plants to avoid excessive growth on the side nearest the light and weak growth on the other side. If you decide to provide supplementary, artificial light, place the fixtures so that the light comes evenly from directly above the plant.

Photoperiodism is the plant's innate programming to its environment. Plants perform best in a rhythmic cycle of light and darkness that closely resembles that of their original habitat. For many plants, the length of the days and nights determines the time they take to reach maturity. Some plants flower when the days are long (14 hours or more). Other plants, known as short-day plants, flower when days are short and they receive at least 14 hours of darkness while their flower buds are setting. Most plants, however, bloom without regard to the length of the day, provided there is a cycle of day and night.

Plants depend on light for their survival. Light is as essential to them as food is for humans. For that reason, it is important to study the light available at the plant station before shopping for a plant.

Light Categories

Plants are quite adaptable to varying light levels. They can, for example, survive and even grow at light levels well below the optimum range, though they won't flower under such circumstances. At very low light levels, however, plants will gradually die. Given sufficient light, plants will live off their energy reserves for a time; then as these expire, they will be unable to absorb sufficient energy to recuperate from their losses.

There are five commonly used categories for defining plant light conditions. Read the descriptions of the categories and determine which one is closest to the light level in each plant station you've identified in your home, then purchase plants accordingly. It is always easier to use plants adapted to your light levels than to try to adapt your conditions to suit the needs of your plants.

Low light   Low light is light shade, a position well back from the nearest window. There is enough light to read by without too much strain, but no direct sunlight. Some plants can survive for a while at even lower levels than this, but they will not grow. Few plants thrive in low light; at best, they tolerate it.

Moderate light Moderate light is average indoor light, neither sunny nor shady. Most foliage plants will adapt well to this level of light, but few plants will bloom in it. A position directly in front of a north window or slightly back from an east or a west one would get moderate light.

Bright indirect light Bright indirect light is an all-purpose level at which both foliage and flowering plants thrive, although flowering plants will bloom more profusely with some direct sunlight. Bright indirect light is found in a northeast or northwest window that receives a few hours of early morning or late afternoon sun and is well lit the rest of the day. The same effect can be obtained in sunnier windows by moving plants back from the light or drawing sheer curtains across the window during the hottest part of the day.

Some direct sunlight Some direct sunlight is direct sunlight for between two and five hours in the morning or afternoon, but not the full strength of midday sun. Usually this is the light found directly in front of an east or west window or a few feet back from a south window. It is the ideal light for many flowering

This Christmas cactus (Schlumbergera × buckleyi) *is typical of plants that need a certain number of hours spent in darkness to bloom again.*

Light Requirements of Various Houseplants

Plants for Low Light
(dim reading-level light)

Botanical Name	Common Name
Aglaonema modestum	Chinese evergreen
Aspidistra elatior	Cast-iron plant
Asplenium nidus	Bird's-nest fern
Dieffenbachia species	Dieffenbachia (dumb-cane)
Dracaena fragrans 'Massangeana'	Cornplant
Lilium longiflorum	Easter lily
Spathiphyllum species	Peace-lily, spatheflower

Plants for Moderate Light
(no direct sunlight)

Botanical Name	Common Name
Acorus gramineus	Miniature flagplant, Japanese sweet flag
Adiantum species	Maidenhair fern
Araucaria heterophylla	Norfolk Island pine
Asplenium bulbiferum	Mother fern
Cissus antarctica	Kangaroo-ivy
Davallia species	Deer's-foot fern, rabbit's-foot fern
Epipremnum aureum	Pothos, Devil's-ivy
Howea forsterana	Kentia palm
Nephrolepis exaltata 'Bostoniensis'	Boston fern, sword fern
Philodendron bipinnatifidum	Twice-cut philodendron
Philodendron hastatum	Spade-leaf philodendron
Philodendron 'Red Emerald'	Red Emerald philodendron
Philodendron scandens oxycardium	Heart-leaf philodendron
Philodendron selloum	Lacy-tree philodendron
Phoenix roebelenii	Pygmy date palm
Pteris species	Table fern, brake fern
Rhapis species	Lady palm

Plants for Bright Indirect Light
(away from direct sunlight, or in a north window)

Botanical Name	Common Name
Aloe species	Aloe
Aphelandra squarrosa**	Zebra-plant
Brassaia actinophylla	Schefflera
Ceropegia species	Rosary vine, hearts-entangled
Coleus × hybridus	Coleus
Dizygotheca elegantissima	False-aralia
Episcia species	Episcias, flame-violets
Fatsia japonica	Japanese aralia
Gibasis species	Tahitian bridal-veil
Ficus species	Ficus, fig
Hippeastrum species	Amaryllis
Mitriostigma axillare	African gardenia
Paphiopedilum	Lady's-slipper
Pellaea rotundifolia	Button fern
Phalaenopsis	Moth-orchid
Rhipsalis species	Chain cactus
Saintpaulia species**	African violet
Schlumbergera species	Christmas cactus, Thanksgiving cactus
Vriesea species	Vriesea

Plants for Some Direct Sun
(curtain-filtered sunlight from a south, east, or west window)

Botanical Name	Common Name
Abutilon species	Flowering-maple, Chinese-lantern
Aeschynanthus species	Lipstick-plant, basket vine
Asparagus species	Asparagus fern
Beaucarnea recurvata	Elephantfoot tree, ponytail-palm
Begonia species	Begonia
Caladium species	Caladium
Camellia species	Camellia
Clivia miniata	Kaffir-lily
Columnea species	Columnea
Crassula argentea	Jade plant
Cryptanthus species	Earthstar
Cyclamen species*	Cyclamen
Euphorbia pulcherrima	Poinsettia
Ficus species	Ficus, fig
Hydrangea macrophylla	Hydrangea
Impatiens species	Impatiens, busy-lizzy
Platycerium bifurcatum	Staghorn fern
Polypodium aureum	Golden polypody fern, bear's-paw fern, hare's-foot fern
Primula species	Primrose
Rhododendron species*	Azalea, rhododendron
Sedum morganianum	Donkey's-tail, burro's-tail
Senecio rowleyanus	String-of-beads
Streptocarpus species	Cape primrose

Plants for Full Sun
(4 or more hours of direct sunlight)

Botanical Name	Common Name
Aechmea species	Living-vaseplant
Agave species	Century plant
Ananas species	Pineapple
Billbergia species	Vaseplant
Calliandra species	Calliandra, powder-puff, flame bush
Cephalocereus senilis	Oldman cactus
Chrysanthemum × morifolium*	Florist's chrysanthemum
Codiaeum variegatum	Croton
Dyckia species	Dyckia
Echeveria species	Echeveria, hen and chicks
Echinopsis species	Urchin cactus
× Fatshedera lizei**	Tree-ivy, aralia-ivy
Gymnocalycium	Chin cactus, spider cactus
Kalanchoe species*	Kalanchoe
Lithops species	Living-stones
Mammillaria species	Pincushion cactus
Opuntia species	Opuntia, bunny-ears
Cattleya** species	Orchid
Dendrobium** species	Orchid
Oncidium** species	Dancing-lady
Pelargonium species	Geranium
Rosa hybrids*	Miniature roses

* Needs full sun to initiate flower buds; bright indirect light will suffice when in flower
** Needs full sun in winter and curtain-filtered sunlight in summer

plants, herbs, and vegetables as well as most cacti and succulents, but it's too bright for all but a few foliage plants.

Full sun   Full sun is more than four or five hours of direct sunlight daily. An unshaded window facing due south during the summer months would receive full sun. Few plants thrive in full sun because of the intense heat, although cacti and succulents tolerate it well. Full sun is easily softened to an ideal light by installing sheer curtains or by moving plants back several feet from the window.

Light Intensity

The farther one travels from the equator, the greater the influence the seasons have on light intensity. In northern climates, for example, there is no equivalent to full sun during the winter months. The brightest winter light is only equal to some direct sunlight or even bright indirect light. At such latitudes, sun-loving plants need the sunniest possible position during the winter months.

The time of year also affects light intensities in other ways. Keep in mind that winter sunlight reaches farther into south-facing rooms than summer sunlight does because of the low angle of the sun. Plants that receive a few hours of direct sunlight in the middle of a room in winter may need to be closer to a window in summer to receive adequate light.

Objects in the light path also affect light intensity. A south-facing window may receive only bright indirect light or some direct sunlight if it is shaded by nearby buildings or trees or an overhanging roof. Placing objects in the light path is an effective way of gaining shade. Sun-loving plants near a window will moderate the amount of light reaching plants set farther back in the room. Screens on windows, doors, or porches reduce light by at least 30 percent. A white house next door or a light-colored cement driveway will reflect sunlight, increasing the intensity of the light the rooms receive. Snow also reflects a great deal of light, especially on a sunny day.

How can you tell whether your plant is getting the right amount of light? Just watch its reactions! If new growth is thin and pale and seems to stretch toward the light, the plant is suffering from a lack of light. Move it to a spot where it will receive better illumination. If the

plant wilts rapidly or is yellowish in color, and the new growth is unusually compact, the plant is getting too much light. Move it back from the light source. If the plant looks good but doesn't flower as it should, it is probably getting sufficient light for good foliage growth but not enough light for flowering. Moving it just a little closer to the window is probably all that's required.

Types of Artificial Light

Choices in artificial light have changed greatly in the past few years. Once you were limited to standard incandescent lighting; now you can choose among incandescent, fluorescent, high-intensity discharge (HID), and halogen lights.

Incandescent lights   Incandescent light is the kind of light most often used in the home. It is not well balanced in light quality, offering mostly red light and very little blue light. Even

A sheer curtain will soften the full direct sunlight from a south-facing window.

The supplemental artificial lights in this room add a touch of nighttime drama while ensuring that the plants receive enough light to flourish.

specially developed incandescent plant lights, whose light quality has been improved for plant growth, are weak in blue rays. Incandescent light is best used as supplemental light in areas where plants receive some natural light. The advantage of incandescent plant lights over regular incandescent bulbs is that they reflect heat away from the plant, which means that you can place the plant closer to the light source. All incandescent lights are inefficient, however, giving off much of their energy as heat; and they need frequent replacement.

Fluorescent lights Fluorescent lights are more efficient than incandescent lights. They convert most of the energy they receive into light rather than heat, so you can place plants within an inch or so of the light source with no danger of burning them. Fluorescents also give off a light more closely balanced in blue and red rays than do incandescent lights. It is quite easy to grow plants under fluorescent lights in areas where there is no natural sunlight at all.

Although most plants will grow perfectly well under ordinary cool-white or warm-white fluorescent tubes, the full-spectrum fluorescent plant lights give off a more perfectly balanced light quality. Use the full-spectrum on plants that do not bloom well under ordinary fluorescents, such as some orchids, as well as on plants that prefer full sun.

To create a light garden with fluorescent lights, set plants so that their upper leaves are 6 to 12 inches from the light source. Place plants requiring full sun closer to the lights than plants preferring moderate light. The basic fixture is a two-tube, 4-foot lamp. This lights a growing space approximately 2 feet wide and 4 feet long—enough for a small indoor garden. For plants preferring full sun, use four-tube lamps; they give off a greater intensity of light. Many people use tiers of plant lights so that they can grow a great many plants in a small space. Fluorescent light gardens are available commercially but are easy to build if you have basic woodworking skills.

The main disadvantage of fluorescent lights is that the intensity of the light diminishes rapidly the farther they are from the plants. Consequently, the top of a tall plant may be well lit while its lower leaves are in deep shade. For that reason, fluorescent lights give better results with low, spreading plants than upright ones.

High-intensity discharge lights HID lamps are powerful, extremely intense lights. They were originally developed for greenhouses, to supply light as intense as full sun, but they can be adapted to indoor use. HID lamps, such as mercury lamps and high-pressure sodium lights, are so powerful that a single lamp can illuminate an entire indoor garden. However, the extreme intensity of the light they provide, as well as the heat they produce, make them unsuitable for normal home conditions: They are simply too bright and too hot for human comfort. Some people do use HID lamps to grow sun-loving plants like vegetables in the basement, attic, or other dedicated plant room. In such cases, a complete ventilation system is necessary to vent the heat they produce. Be careful not to spray water on HID lamps; they are extremely fragile when hot.

Halogen lights   Halogen lights are miniature versions of HID lamps. Currently fashionable in home and office settings, they give off light of exceptional quality, making them good choices for growing indoor plants. They also have the advantage of dramatically drawing attention to the plants they illuminate with such clear intensity. However, they give off a great deal of heat and will burn the leaves of plants that are too close. Because halogen lamps produce beams that are quite narrow, they are most suitable for individual plants or small groups of plants.

CHOOSING GROWING MEDIA

The medium in which a plant grows serves three main purposes. It acts as a support, keeping the plant from falling over; it stores water

The bright light of this halogen lamp spotlights the dramatic form of the medicine plant (Aloe vera) *and provides exceptional light quality for the plant's growth.*

and nutrients; and it provides sufficient air circulation to keep the roots well oxygenated. Any medium that supplies those three basic needs will give good results.

In the past, garden soils were brought indoors and pasteurized for use in pots, but the results were often poor. That's because growing a plant in a pot indoors involves conditions (limited root space, little action from soil organisms, and so on) that are quite different from the conditions in the ground outdoors. Typical garden soils, as light and airy as they may appear at first, quickly become as compact as cement in a pot indoors. Compaction cuts off oxygen supplies to the plant roots, and without oxygen roots quickly rot. Indoor growers learned with time to amend garden soil with products such as sand, leaf mold, or charcoal to keep it as well aerated as possible.

Today's potting mixes often contain no true soil at all; they go under the name *peat-based mixes* or *soilless mixes*. Typically they are composed of peat moss or some other partially decomposed plant material, such as fine fir bark, and inorganic elements such as perlite and vermiculite. They offer all the qualities that garden soil offers outdoors: They provide good support for roots and excellent retention of water and minerals; and they are also quite porous, allowing easy circulation of oxygen. Their chief disadvantage is that they are almost totally lacking in natural nutrients, so plants will not thrive unless small amounts of fertilizer are added with each watering. Also, since even the best soilless mix becomes compact with time, it needs to be replaced every year or so.

Measuring Acidity and Alkalinity

An important factor in the composition of any growing medium is its acidity or alkalinity. Acidity and alkalinity are measured in terms of pH. The pH scale ranges from 0 to 14, with 7 being neutral. A pH reading higher than 7 is alkaline, and one lower than 7 is acid. Highly acid mixes cause yellowing and leaf drop. Alkaline soil can cause stunted growth and loss of leaf color.

Most packaged potting mixes are slightly acid; they have a pH of about 6.5 to 6.8, which is ideal for most plants. The mixes suggested here include dolomite lime to raise the pH to a similar level. For acid-loving plants (azaleas, gardenias, citrus, and so on), prepare the mixes without the dolomite lime. Many cacti and succulents prefer a neutral or slightly alkaline soil, which you can easily provide by adding extra lime.

Preparing Your Own Growing Media

Good growing media are usually available ready-made wherever plants are sold. However, the mixes tend to be general-purpose ones and may not be well suited to the type of plants that you are growing. If they are not suitable, you can adapt them to your needs by adding one or two ingredients or you can start from scratch and make your own mix.

The ingredients for a homemade houseplant mix are the same as those found in commercial mixes. Each plays a specific role in helping houseplants grow and flourish.

Pasteurized garden loam Many growers like to add some garden soil to soilless mixes. It makes the mix heavier, providing tall plants with more support; and it contains certain nutrients, reducing the need for regular fertilizing. Any soil of garden origin must be pasteurized before use to destroy soil-borne pests and diseases. Do this by thoroughly moistening small quantities and baking them at 200° F for 30 minutes. (Be forewarned: Many soils smell decidedly unpleasant while baking.) Alternatively, you can purchase an already pasteurized mix. The disadvantage of garden soils of any sort is a lack of consistency in their quality: You simply never know what you are getting or how it will react when compacted into a pot.

Peat moss Made up of various types of partially decomposed bog plants, peat moss is the basic element of most modern potting mixes. Even those indoor gardeners who prefer to grow their plants in soil usually include a fairly large proportion of peat moss in their mixes. It adds lightness to a mix and improves water retention; and since it expands when moist and contracts when dry, it literally pulls air into the soil. The main disadvantages of peat moss are its tendencies to compact with time and become increasingly acid. It contains almost no nutrients. The most popular type for potting mixes is Canadian sphagnum peat.

Basic potting mixes are available prepackaged from your local nursery or garden center. Shown left to right are a mix for orchids, a general houseplant mix, and a mix for cacti and succulents.

Vermiculite   Vermiculite is expanded mica; it looks like little flakes of gold. Because of its excellent soil aeration properties, it has become a basic element of most soilless mixes. It can absorb several times its weight in water and minerals, and releases them slowly. Its main disadvantage is a tendency to become compact with time. The fine and medium grades are most popular. Use only horticultural vermiculite; construction-grade vermiculite sometimes contains harmful impurities.

Perlite   Perlite is a white, expanded volcanic rock that helps to maintain good aeration in a mix. Like vermiculite, it absorbs excess minerals and water and releases them over time. Unlike vermiculite, it does not compact significantly with time, making it a choice ingredient for a mix that will be used to pot mature plants. Coarse to medium grades are preferable. Perlite tends to rise to the surface when watered.

Charcoal   Charcoal is often absent from commercial mixes, but it is worthwhile to add some to your potting mixes even if you don't usually mix your own soil. It acts as a buffer in the potting mix, absorbing potentially harmful excess minerals as well as toxins resulting from decomposition. Use only horticultural- or aquarium-grade charcoal, and sift it first to remove the dust. Never add barbecue charcoal to a potting mix.

Sphagnum moss   Sphagnum moss is a bog moss used for plants that require a very airy yet humid growing medium. Long-strand sphagnum moss is sometimes sold in living (still green) form; more often it is dried and golden brown. Before using it, soak it in warm water, and use it only with some form of lime to counteract its high acidity. Because sphagnum moss has natural fungicidal properties, a milled form is often used in seed mixtures to help prevent damping-off, a fungus that resembles mildew. Milled sphagnum moss is too fine for use in regular potting mixes.

Bark   Fine grades of ground tree bark are sometimes used as a substitute for peat moss. Coarser grades are a common ingredient in epiphytic mixes used for orchids and bromeliads because they provide excellent aeration.

Styrofoam   Styrofoam beads are sometimes used as substitutes for perlite, although they don't have all its desirable qualities. They do help aerate the mix, but they don't absorb excess water and minerals and release them as needed. Styrofoam is also so light that it floats to the surface when watered. Styrofoam peanuts, a common packaging material, are occasionally used in epiphytic mixes.

Calcined clay   Composed of chunks of kiln-hardened clay, calcined clay is most widely available in the form of unscented cat litter. It adds aeration and drainage to a mix and absorbs excess water. It makes a good substitute for vermiculite and perlite when a heavier mix is desired. Always sift it to remove the dust before adding it to a mix.

Coarse sand   Used mainly in succulent mixes, coarse sand adds weight to a medium and improves drainage. Use only horticultural or washed sand.

Dolomite lime   A white powder, dolomite lime is added in small quantities to mixes, especially peat-based ones, to reduce their acidity.

Mix-and-Match Potting Media

Many people prefer mixing their own potting media to ensure just the right combination of ingredients. Below are formulas for some of the most popular mixes.

Basic Soilless Mix

This is a general-purpose soilless mix that is well suited to most kinds of indoor plants.

> *1 quart coarse peat moss*
> *1 quart medium-grade vermiculite*
> *1 quart medium-grade perlite*
> *3 tablespoons dolomite lime*
> *1 cup sifted horticultural charcoal*

Soil-Based Mix

This heavier mix is especially useful for plants you don't want to repot annually.

> *1 part pasteurized garden loam*
> *1 part basic soilless mix or commercial soilless mix*

Epiphytic Mix

This mix is suitable for orchids, bromeliads, and other air plants, which derive much of their moisture and nutrients from the air and rain.

> *1 quart long-strand sphagnum moss*
> *1 quart coarse bark*
> *1 quart coarse-grade perlite*
> *1 tablespoon dolomite lime*
> *1 cup sifted horticultural charcoal*

Cactus Mix

This mix is ideal for cacti and succulents, and also for top-heavy plants, which need a weighty soil.

> *2 quarts pasteurized garden loam*
> *1 quart coarse sand*
> *1 quart calcined clay*
> *2 tablespoons dolomite lime*
> *½ cup sifted horticultural charcoal*

PROVIDING THE RIGHT TEMPERATURE, HUMIDITY, AND AIR CIRCULATION

The environment also contributes to plant health. Although you may not be able to duplicate the native habitat of a plant in your home, paying attention to the temperature, humidity, and air circulation in your home will help your plants flourish.

Temperature

Temperature, in concert with light, humidity, and air circulation, affects plant metabolism. Most indoor plants adapt to normal indoor temperatures (55° to 75° F). At night, they almost all benefit from at least a five-degree drop in temperature, which gives them a chance to recover from any rapid water loss that may have taken place during the day. Overnight, the roots continue to take in water, correcting any water deficits in the leaf cells.

Few houses have uniform temperatures in each room. Use a thermometer to check the temperature in different locations of your house, and even at various plant stations within the same room.

Even indoors, temperatures change with the seasons. In winter, home heating and cold drafts from windows and doors can cause widely fluctuating temperatures. In summer, the temperature at a south-facing window can soar. Though most plants appreciate changes in temperature, because such changes are natural to their native habitat, some seasonal temperature changes are severe enough to warrant moving plants, especially those growing on windowsills, to a different location.

Tropical plants native to areas with high temperatures and humidity—episcias, prayer-plants (*Maranta*), and bougainvilleas, for example—may grow best in a room that contains an appliance that vents wet heat, such as a dishwasher, clothes dryer, or humidifier. In a cool room, tropical plants can thrive if the soil is heated by electric heating cables or propagation mats (for more information on these, see page 106). Cold-loving plants (55° to 60° F days, 50° F nights), such as cyclamens, camellias, azaleas, and some orchids, do well in rooms where there is no bright direct sunlight to raise the temperature. And certain plants require specialized growing conditions, such as a permanent greenhouse environment or an unheated room for a short resting period.

Humidity

Humidity is the moisture content of the air. It is expressed as relative humidity: a percentage of the maximum amount of water vapor the air can hold at a given temperature.

Nearly all houseplants grow best in a relative humidity of 50 percent or higher, but this level is difficult to attain in dry climates and indoors in winter. In winter, home heating robs the air of moisture; humidities as low as 4 to 10 percent are common. Some areas of the house are naturally more humid than others. Plants grown in such moisture-rich areas as bathrooms and kitchens benefit from the increased humidity.

A cool-vapor humidifier can increase the humidity considerably on even the coldest days, making the air more comfortable for both people and plants. You can move portable units from room to room or install a humidifier as part of the central heating system. The simplest method for humidifying the air around plants is to use pebble trays: waterproof trays or saucers filled with pebbles, perlite, or vermiculite. Fill these trays with water to just below the surface of the material and place the plants on top. Check that the bottom of the pot is not touching the water; if it is, you are risking root rot. As the water evaporates it fills the surrounding air with moisture. Add water to the tray as necessary. Humidifying trays are strongly recommended for plants growing under artificial lights.

You may also raise the humidity level by grouping plants together. The combined transpiration from a group of plants raises the humidity around those plants. The leaves will catch and hold the transpired moisture. Leave enough room between the plants to encourage air circulation, which helps prevent disease.

Another popular method of increasing humidity, especially for orchids and ferns, is misting. The spray from a mister should create a fine cloud of moisture. Mist in the morning so that the moisture will evaporate during the day.

A pebble tray filled with water to just below the tops of the rocks, never any higher, will supply humidity for the plant above it.

Tabs inserted into the soil steadily release fertilizer over a period of time.

Leaves that are moist for long periods are particularly prone to disease. Fuzzy-leaved plants, such as African violets (*Saintpaulia*), should not be misted; they will develop water spots if the tops of the leaves become wet.

Misting, unless done several times a day, raises the humidity only temporarily. In dry rooms moisture evaporates quickly. Humidifying the air and adequate watering are the only ways to ensure that plants have sufficient moisture.

Air Circulation

Plants enjoy fresh air as much as people do. Soft breezes of warm, humid air supply oxygen and moisture, keeping the plant healthy. Plants that are cramped together or placed in an environment where air does not circulate are more likely to develop fungal diseases.

At the same time, drafts also can harm plants. Dry air movement over leaves can cause moisture stress and leaf burn, especially in direct sunlight. Sudden changes in air movement and temperature can send plants into shock. Be especially careful with plants that are near a window, particularly during winter.

Air pollution affects plants in a number of ways. Fumes from burning propane or butane gas may cause leaves to yellow and leaves and flower buds to drop. Fumes from burning natural gas are not harmful to plants.

Dust and dirt from the air accumulate on plant leaves, clogging the stomata and slowing growth. To keep plants growing well, give smooth-leaved plants a shower once a month or a good rinse (see page 39). Between showers and for fuzzy-leaved plants, such as African violets (*Saintpaulia*), you can gently wipe off the dust with a soft rag, brush, or feather duster, taking care not to harm the leaves.

FERTILIZING

Photosynthesis provides plants with the sugar and other carbohydrates they need for energy. Fertilizers provide the nutritive minerals they require for healthy growth. Plants that need to be fertilized exhibit slow growth, pale leaves, weak stems, small or nonexistent flowers, or dropped leaves.

Fertilizers come in many different formulations to suit various types of plants. The labels usually list three numbers. These are, in order, the percentages of nitrogen, phosphorus, and potassium that make up the fertilizer. Nitrogen, phosphorus, and potassium are the three major nutrients that plants need. A fertilizer labeled 12-6-6 is 12 percent nitrogen, 6 percent phosphate, and 6 percent potash.

Nitrogen primarily enriches the greenness of the foliage and promotes stem growth. Phosphorus encourages flowering and root growth. Potassium contributes to stem strength and disease resistance. Fertilizers formulated for flowering plants usually contain less nitrogen and more phosphorous and potassium. You can also find specialized fertilizers for some plant groups, such as orchids.

In addition to the three nutrients, plants need three secondary nutrients—sulfur, calcium, and magnesium—and minute quantities of iron, zinc, manganese, copper, chlorine, boron, and molybdenum. These latter are called micronutrients, or trace minerals or elements.

Fertilizers are available in many forms: water-soluble pellets, powders, liquids, dry tablets, time-release pellets, and sticks to insert in the soil. Their value and strength vary widely; if you have questions, consult the houseplant specialist who sold you the plant. Before applying fertilizers, always read the label first and follow the directions carefully. Remember that more is not better: Excess fertilizer can burn roots and leaves.

Most fertilizers on the market have been formulated for use once a month, but small biweekly doses are safer than large monthly doses. If monthly doses are recommended, reduce the suggested amount by one half and feed biweekly instead. Most foliage plants need far less fertilizer than flowering plants. Fertilize foliage plants at half strength between March and October. During the winter months reduce the applications or stop fertilizing the plants altogether.

Before deciding that a plant needs extra fertilizer, review its other care requirements to determine whether they are being met. If a regularly fertilized plant isn't growing, it's likely that the plant is dormant or sick. The worst time to fertilize is when a plant is ailing. Sickly plants will decline even more rapidly if heavily fertilized, and may even die.

Overfertilization is a common error, particularly with plants on maintenance rather than growth programs. Dormant plants do not require the same amounts of fertilizer as plants growing actively. Too much fertilizer will cause leaf burn, poorly shaped leaves, or a white crust on the pots and the surface of the growing medium; too-frequent fertilization may cause deformed growth.

If you accidentally overfertilize a plant, thorough watering should solve the problem. Thorough watering will also help wash out accumulated fertilizer salts, which can build up

Cacti and Succulents

Succulents, of which cacti are a part, exhibit a wide variety of colors, shapes, textures, and sizes. They are the camels of the plant kingdom; their well-developed water conservation techniques can carry them through periods of drought. Not all succulents are native to arid areas. Some come from the tropics, where long dry seasons are followed by a short season of heavy rain.

As a group, succulents are easy to grow if their general preferences are followed. A clay pot just large enough to accommodate the plant without overcrowding its roots is best. If a small plant is placed in too large a pot, its roots may rot in unabsorbed water. Bonsai containers are splendid for displaying succulents, and the drainage holes are the right size for allowing unabsorbed water to drain.

Most succulents need to dry out between waterings. Clay and other porous materials make it easier to control the moisture level, although you can use plastic pots if you water the plants less frequently. Water quality is especially important for succulents, which are sensitive to mineral salts.

During their growing season, cacti and succulents need watering whenever the soil begins to dry out. During dormancy, however, water sparingly (just enough to keep the roots alive). Don't let them dehydrate; water before foliage and stems go limp and shrivel. In springtime, when plants show signs of fresh growth, begin thorough watering again. Set the pots in a pan of water and allow them to "drink" until the soil is just moist on top.

Fertilize succulents only during the growing period, and dilute to a quarter of the recommended strength for the fertilizer. Feed in small amounts about every third watering, stopping as soon as plants cease their seasonal growth.

Good air circulation is crucial, since stagnant air encourages mealybugs. Keep the plants cool at night but not cold, and place them where they will receive strong light during the day unless, like the tropical cacti, they prefer filtered sunlight.

Fertilizer burn is often the reason for brown leaf tips.

Leach out excess salts accumulated from fertilizers and water.

watered, the year around. When plants are fertilized this way, growth is more symmetrical and leaf color and size are also more even. However, you must use a fertilizer formulated especially for this purpose. If you do not, you risk overfertilizing and damaging the roots. And remember, plants that require less watering during rest periods will also require less fertilizer during those times.

Foliar Feeding

In their native habitats plants absorb nutrients from rain and bird droppings falling onto their leaves. In a home environment they will absorb specially formulated fertilizers sprayed or misted onto the foliage. Use only fertilizers recommended for foliar application, which are available at garden stores, and follow the directions on the label. Indoor gardeners often apply trace elements as foliar sprays.

Foliar feeding acts quickly but lasts a relatively short time. It is best used as a supplement to fertilizers applied directly to the soil.

GROOMING

People like plants because they symbolize life and vitality. Yellow leaves and brown tips can quickly destroy that image. Houseplants demand regular grooming, trimming, and pruning to keep them manageable in size and attractive in shape. Good grooming also reduces the possibility of disease and helps flowering plants produce superior blossoms.

Cleaning

Dust and dirt on leaves keep light from reaching the leaf pores, harming the plant as well as making it unsightly. Cleaning the plant allows the leaves to breathe and also helps rid them of insect eggs and mites. Dampen a cloth or soft sponge in mild soapy water to remove grime from smooth-leaved plants. Support the leaf in one hand while gently wiping away from the stem. Avoid cleaning new growth.

Use a dry, soft hairbrush or paintbrush to clean the fuzzy leaves of plants such as African violet (*Saintpaulia*) and velvetplant (*Gynura aurantiaca*). Plants with fuzzy leaves do not react well to having water on their leaves. For large plants with many tiny leaves, such as weeping fig (*Ficus benjamina*), a feather duster—especially one made with ostrich feathers—is ideal.

and harm the plant. Salt buildup shows as a whitish deposit on the outside of clay pots or as salt burn on the edges of leaves. The condition is a serious one but can be remedied by percolating water through—leaching—the soil. Place the plant in a sink, tub, or pail and water it several times, letting the water drain each time. In mild weather, you can place the plant outdoors and water it with a hose, a technique especially useful for large plants. If salts have become a problem, they will not leach out in one day; you may have to repeat the process weekly for several weeks. As a last resort, gently wash the old soil from the roots and repot the plant in fresh soil.

Constant Feeding

Many plants, including African violets (*Saintpaulia*), can be fertilized on a constant-feed program; in other words, every time they are

Exercise caution with all cleaning materials, especially dusters, to avoid transferring pests from an infested plant to a clean one. To avoid contamination, clean the cloths, sponges, and dusters in warm, soapy water or a 1:10 solution of household bleach and water and allow them to dry before using them again. You can also spray them with a disinfectant after use. Let them air out for a day or so after disinfecting them, to avoid any plant damage.

The leaves of certain plants look better with a little extra sheen. There are leaf shine products on the market, but they should be used with care and in moderation.

Trimming

Once a leaf has turned entirely yellow, it will never become green again. It should be removed to improve both the look of the plant and its general health. When the tip of a leaf turns yellow or brown, trim away the discolored area for the same reasons. When cutting, use sharp shears and follow the original shape of the leaf, taking as little green, vital material as possible. Small discolored leaves should be pinched off at the base of their stems.

Yellow and brown leaves are not always signs that the plant is ailing. Some attrition is part of the natural growth cycle of most plants.

Pinching

Pinching off a young stem tip encourages most plants to branch out below the pinch and become bushier and healthier. For example, a young coleus plant started from a seed or cutting must be pinched during its active growth period or one stem will grow straight up and the plant will become gangly and weak. To avoid this, use your thumb and forefinger to nip off the growing tip as soon as the plant has four to six leaves. Dormant buds will spring into active growth, producing additional stems. After two or three weeks, pinch the tips of these new stems.

Pinching works well for most plants, but is especially recommended for soft-stemmed plants, such as certain begonia species and young geraniums (*Pelargonium*).

Pruning

Pruning is removing young, woody stems. When part of a plant is removed, the energy invested in sustaining that part is directed

Top: Wiping or brushing off a plant's leaves removes dust and dirt, which can dull the plant's appearance, and helps stop the spread of diseases and pests. Center: To improve the look of a plant and its general health, trim off any yellow tips of leaves or a leaf that has turned entirely yellow. Bottom: Pinching encourages soft-stemmed plants to branch out and become fuller. Pinch the top of each new branch as it forms.

toward the rest of the plant. This explains why a sickly plant may be revived by pruning, and why flowering plants may be encouraged to bloom. Pruning requires care and some basic knowledge, but it is not difficult. With careful shaping you can create a compact, cared-for, topiary look from shapeless, random growth.

Before you make the first cut, consider the effect you'd like to achieve. Removing a stem at its point of origin will force new growth in the remaining stems or from the base of the plant. Cutting off a stem above a leaf will encourage one or more new growth tips to appear near the cut and make the plant denser. With a sharp pair of small hand-pruners, make cuts on branching plants just above a node or just above a leaf to avoid unsightly bare stems all over the plant. Make the cuts at a slight angle so that the cut surface faces inward, toward the center of the plant.

Vining plants, such as pothos (*Epiprem-num aureum*), grape-ivy (*Cissus rhombi-folia*), and wandering-Jew (*Tradescantia* or *Zebrina* species), require a different pruning method. To achieve both long stems and full-ness at the base, allow just a few vines to grow to full length and pinch all the others well back. Pinching induces branching and will help to keep the plant looking lush. Periodically, vining plants should be cut back severely. Make cuts just above leaf buds or branches, and save the cuttings for rooting. For a particu-larly full, healthy look, root the cuttings in the same pot as the parent plant.

Sometimes an old though still healthy plant loses its lower foliage. To hide the bare stem, place the plant in a large container and add several smaller plants of the same species—or a ground cover, such as pothos (*Epipremnum aureum*)—to fill the empty space.

POTTING AND TRANSPLANTING

After months or perhaps a year or more of good care, houseplants grow too large for their origi-nal containers and need repotting to stay healthy and continue growing vigorously. Plan to repot your plants periodically as part of a regular maintenance program. The telltale signs of a pot-bound plant will help you decide when it's time to repot.

If a plant seems to need enormous amounts of water, it has probably grown too many roots

for its container and needs a larger pot. Long strands of roots coming out of the drainage hole or a rootball that fills the pot completely are signs of this problem.

To see whether the roots are compacted, turn the plant on its side and gently knock the rim of the pot against a solid surface to loosen the rootball. If it doesn't come out, the soil may be too wet. Let it dry a little; then try again. If the roots are massed along the sides of the pot and at the base of the rootball, it is time to repot the plant.

Sometimes a newly purchased plant will need repotting. Plants are often shipped to nurseries in a light shipping soil that dries out quickly and needs frequent fertilization. Many small plants are actually rooted cuttings, and these are often underpotted. If, after a week of adjustment to its new home, a new plant still needs constant watering, repot it into a larger pot and a quality growing medium.

Tall plants, such as ficus, avocado (*Persea americana*), and certain dracaenas, need re-potting when they start to look overgrown; they may topple if they become top heavy. The final, but no less important, reason for repot-ting is that plants in handsome new containers can change the look of a room almost as dra-matically as new furniture.

As a rule, the new pot should be no more than 2 inches larger than the old one. A repot-ted plant will not grow well until its roots begin to fill the container. Also, a greatly enlarged mass of soil with few roots retains too much water, leading to root rot.

Above: Pruning young, woody stems gives a plant a compact, cared-for look and encourages flowering plants to bloom. Opposite, top: Holding the plant securely, tap the plant out of the container. For large plants, you may need help steadying the pot. Opposite, center: Partially fill the new container with planting mix; then position the plant at the height it grew in its previous pot. Firm the soil around the plant and fill the pot with soil. Opposite, bottom: Once you have added the soil, firm it around the plant and water thoroughly.

A second rule of thumb on pot size is that the diameter of the rim should equal one third to one half the height of the plant. Tall, slender plants will grow in small pots, as long as the pots are wide enough to provide a stable base. Vining or trailing plants will also grow well in small pots.

Wet the growing medium before using it, preferably a day in advance. If the medium you are using comes in plastic bags, add tepid water and tie the top of the bag tightly to keep the medium moist. If you are using a homemade mix, scoop some into a plastic bag and moisten it in the same way. Or place the mix in a large bowl, knead in water by hand, and leave it overnight covered with plastic wrap or foil.

About an hour before repotting, water the plant thoroughly. If you are potting into a new clay pot, soak the pot thoroughly (until air bubbles no longer rise from it) to ensure that it will not absorb water from the growing medium.

To remove the plant from its existing pot, turn the plant on its side and gently knock the rim of the pot against a solid surface to loosen it. If it doesn't come out, the soil may be too wet. Let it dry a little; then try again. If the pot is large, lay it on its side and run a sharp knife or spatula around the edge of the pot. Pull the plant out—you may need a second pair of hands to steady the pot.

When transferring a pot-bound plant from a round container, you may notice that the roots have circled around the inside of the container. Prune roots that are circling the rootball before transplanting: Make three or four ½-inch-deep cuts from the top of the rootball to the bottom with a sharp knife. The pruning will stimulate new root growth and help the roots penetrate the new mix surrounding the rootball.

To transplant, partly fill the new container with the planting mix. Place the plant at the height it grew in its previous pot. Firm the soil around the rootball; then fill the container with soil. Tamp the planting mix with your fingers, especially near the edges of the container. Water thoroughly, and keep the roots moist until they have spread into the surrounding soil. Repot a plant as quickly as possible so that the roots do not dry out.

Occasionally a plant will need additional nourishment rather than repotting, especially if it performs better when pot bound. Such plants will benefit from a top dressing. To top-dress a plant, scrape off the top 1 or 2 inches of growing medium with a fork or small rake. Then fill the pot to its original level with fresh potting mixture, tamping it firmly.

CHOOSING POTS AND CONTAINERS

Pots directly influence the growth, appearance, and needs of the plants they contain. They can be as casual as a coconut shell or a repainted coffee can or as formal as a glazed bonsai planter. Plastic and cloth bags, old whiskey and wine barrels, stoneware bowls, and pieces of driftwood can all be converted into unusual plant containers. The following containers are the most common.

Plastic Pots

Plastic pots come in any number of shapes and sizes (generally ranging from 2 to 18 inches in diameter) and are lighter and less expensive than clay pots. Plants in plastic pots need watering less often than plants in clay pots; since plastic pots are not porous, they retain moisture much longer. However, since air cannot move through the pot walls, plastic pots require growing media with excellent drainage. Before reusing plastic pots, scrub them clean with a stiff brush and warm water. If you want, you can also soak them in a 1:10 solution of household bleach and water.

Clay Pots

The standard clay pot is both functional and attractive. It comes in the same shapes and sizes as plastic pots and has a drainage hole in

Pots directly influence the growth, appearance, and needs of the plants they contain. Clay, ceramic, and plastic containers in a wide variety of shapes and sizes are readily available in plant stores.

the bottom. Clay saucers may be sold with the pots or separately.

The unglazed porous clay allows air and water to move through the pot wall. Clay pots, therefore, should be soaked in a basin of water for several hours before being used. Otherwise, the dry clay will absorb water from the potting soil, robbing the new plantings of moisture.

Because they are porous, clay saucers will eventually create water stains on surfaces where they're placed. To protect your furniture and floors, cut a round piece of cork ½ inch thick to fit beneath the saucer, or use a thick cork coaster. A more practical solution is simply not to use clay saucers; instead, choose moisture-proof plastic or glazed ceramic.

Before reusing clay pots, scrub them clean with a stiff brush and warm water to eliminate salt buildup on the pot. To sterilize them, run them through a dishwasher or put them into an oven for one hour at 180° F. Or soak them in a 1:10 solution of household bleach and water.

Glazed Pottery Pots

Glazed pottery containers can be highly decorative, lending a distinctive touch to almost any decor. The wide array of sizes and designs includes bonsai pots and trays that are particularly attractive for miniature landscapes or bulbs. Some glazed containers have no drainage holes; these are best used as cachepots (see page 57) for slightly smaller clay or plastic pots.

Woven Baskets

Woven baskets look attractive, but they can rot quickly from contact with moisture. Some have plastic liners to alleviate the moisture problem, but then they lack drainage. For these reasons, baskets, too, are best used as cachepots (see page 57), covering a more utilitarian grow pot. Even with an interior saucer or plastic liner to catch moisture, wet baskets can cause extensive moisture damage to surfaces. To avoid such damage, place baskets on plastic mats or on cork pads.

Window Boxes and Wood Planters

Planters made of rot-resistant redwood or cypress, though not as popular for houseplants as other types of planters, can fill a decorative niche. Because the construction of wood planters

Plants and baskets are natural companions. Here, the baskets and pots blend together in a pleasing mix of tans, browns, and beiges while the bright yellow orchid provides an accent note.

may not be as watertight as that of plastic, clay, or ceramic containers, they are probably best used as cachepots (see the next section), concealing the grow pots and drainage trays placed inside. Orchids and other epiphytic plants grow extremely well in wood planters because the potting mix dries out rapidly.

Plastic- and enamel-coated metal window boxes, which are lightweight and available in a variety of colors, are also available. The best of these have drainage holes. On an indoor windowsill they should also have matching trays to catch the drained water.

Cachepots and Jardinieres

Plants on a growth program eventually require pots larger than the ones they came in. Once, however, a plant has reached the perfect size for the space it fills, maintenance rather than growth becomes the goal, but the grow pot in which the plant is potted, while ideal for the cultural needs of the plant, may not fit in with the decorating scheme of the room. Then it's time simply to set the pot inside a decorative container, often called a cachepot or jardiniere. Make certain that the container is at least 2 inches higher than the grow pot.

Since the grow pot provides drainage, the outside container need not; it may either be watertight or have a saucer. Put a 1-inch layer of loose material that will not decompose in the bottom of the decorative container; Styrofoam chips and crushed chicken wire are good choices. Set the grow pot in the decorative pot and pack more of the bottom fill material around the sides. To hide the grow pot, spread a mulch of sphagnum moss, Spanish moss, bark chips, or water-polished stones over the surface.

Water the grow pot thoroughly at each watering. The water that drains through into the decorative pot should evaporate. If it doesn't, loosen the top mulch to allow more air into the fill material.

Hanging Planters

Hanging planters add an interesting dimension to a room. They highlight fine architectural details and disguise unattractive ones. They make efficient use of space and avoid monotonous concentration of plants at one level. A trailing plant with its vines cascading over the edges of a planter hung high in the air provides a very graceful effect. However, bear in mind that the vines will cascade only if there is

sufficient top light. Hanging plants flourish where they receive light from above, under skylights or in light wells or solariums.

Hanging pots The simplest hanging planter is a clay or plastic pot suspended by a wire hanger that is clamped on or attached through holes in the pot. Most of these simple planters have saucers built into the container or attached underneath; ones without saucers must be watered in the sink and then drained, or they will drip onto the floor. Choose the hangers that have built-in swivels so that you can rotate every side of the planter toward the sun.

Regular pots can be transformed into hanging planters with a simple string or rope macramé cradle supporting and surrounding both the pot and its saucer. These macramé cradles are available in many plant centers, but they also are simple to make with heavy twine or strong, waterproof nylon cord.

Wood planters Many hanging planters are made of wood. These are attractive but dry out quickly. They are popular for growing orchids and other epiphytic plants, however, because these plants prefer a quick-drying soil.

This squirrel's-foot fern (Davallia mariesii) *looks elegant in its glazed ceramic pot.*

Wire baskets Since draining water will run unimpeded from a wire basket, use this kind of hanging planter only above a masonry floor. Line the basket with coarse, unmilled sphagnum moss and then fill with soil.

Caring for hanging plants Whichever type of hanging planter you use, leave enough watering space at the top. Fill the planter with soil to within ½ inch from the top, not to the rim. In a moss-lined basket, pack sphagnum moss thick and tight around the top inch of the basket to create a watering basin.

A hanging container needs more frequent watering than a pot on the ground or on a windowsill. Exposed to air on all sides, it more quickly loses water to evaporation. Give the soil a thorough soaking whenever you water, or water sparingly several times a day. Hanging planters can be watered without too much extra effort by using a squeeze-type plastic watering bottle designed especially for this purpose.

Hanging plants require vigilant grooming. Remove all spent blooms, and cut back straying shoots. To keep the plants looking full and healthy, grow new young shoots in the same pot by pinning tips or vines to the moss lining or the growing medium with old-fashioned hairpins or paper clips that have been straightened and then bent in the shape of a U. Rotate the planter frequently so that all sides are evenly exposed to the sun.

Self-Watering Containers

Do you consider watering plants part of the enjoyment of indoor gardening, or is it a chore? If you prefer to spend your time enjoying your plants rather than watering them, then self-watering containers are the choice for you.

Self-watering containers have a water reservoir that needs attention only when it gets low, usually every couple of weeks. Since fertilizer is usually added to the water at the same time, feeding and watering become tasks to be done every few weeks instead of every few days. Meanwhile, the pot automatically delivers water at the rate the plant uses it, adjusting the delivery rate to changes in light, humidity, or temperature. Plants in self-watering pots are usually more evenly watered than plants growing in conventional pots.

Self-watering pots operate on the principle of capillary attraction. In the same way that water

will move upward to moisten an entire towel when just the tip dips into the sink, water will move from the reservoir into the potting mix above. For this to work, however, there does need to be a link—a wick of some sort—between the water and the growing medium.

There are many types of self-watering containers. Some have built-in reservoirs. Others are actually two pots: a grow pot and an outer pot or cachepot that fits around the grow pot; the outer pot acts as a reservoir.

Most self-watering containers use a fibrous wick made of a synthetic material (natural fibers rot from constant contact with moisture) to draw water up into the growing medium. In others, the bottom of the grow pot is made of a porous material (often unglazed ceramic), and the water moves through this material and into the potting medium.

The potting medium itself can also act as a wick. In some self-watering containers, the grow pot has deep ridges in its base that descend to the bottom of the reservoir. The ridges are pierced with just a few holes so that water flows in slowly. The narrow column of potting soil filling the ridges is in constant contact with the water in the reservoir and provides moisture to the drier soil above by means of capillary action.

Self-watering pots have different ways of indicating when the reservoir is empty and when it is too full. Some pots show the water

The beams of this attic bathroom provide the perfect support for hanging planters containing columnea and variegated ivy (Cissus). The floor and tub surround also serve as plant stations for the dwarf anthurium (Anthurium scherzeranum) and maidenhair fern (Adiantum).

Self-watering containers are available commercially in a variety of shapes and sizes.

level with a float, often colored red for maximum visibility. Others have a clear plastic gauge along one side of the reservoir. In some, the entire reservoir is made of a transparent material so that you can see the water level even from a distance. The disadvantage of the latter method is that the water is exposed to light, which encourages the growth of unsightly algae.

There are also different ways of adding water to the reservoir. Containers with built-in reservoirs have an opening in the side or on the top into which you can pour the water. If the grow pot is separate from the outer pot, just lift up the grow pot and pour water directly into the reservoir. Never overfill. If the grow pot is touching the water, the roots may rot.

Making Your Own Self-Watering Pot

It is easy to make a self-watering pot on your own. All you need are a potted plant, an empty refrigerator container, and a strand of fiber that can be used as a wick. Polyester yarn makes an excellent wick, as do thin strips of an old nylon stocking.

Cut the wick to 4 to 6 inches in length. Cut a hole in the center of the lid of the refrigerator container, then cut a second hole close to the edge of the lid. Remove the plant from its pot, and insert the wick through one of the drainage holes in the pot. Wind the wick around the bottom of the pot, letting a few inches hang out. (If you don't want to unpot the plant, you can push the wick up into the potting mix through a drainage hole by means of a nut pick

or knitting needle.) Set the pot on the lid of the container so that the end of the wick hangs down through the hole in the center of the lid. Pour water through the second hole to fill the container. Your homemade self-watering pot is complete.

Self-Watering Tips

Although self-watering pots are essentially simple to operate, these few pointers will help you avoid any problems.

• Most wicks need to be primed (premoistened). Soak the wick in water before use. If the grow pot has a porous bottom designed to act as a wick, likewise let it soak in water for two hours before use. After potting the plant, water it from the top the first time to prime that part of the system too.

• If the potting mix is constantly soggy, install a thinner wick. If it is always too dry, install a thicker wick or several wicks.

• Use only soilless mixes in self-watering pots. Garden soil tends to compact quickly when kept constantly moist.

• Never put a drainage layer of gravel or pot shards in the bottom of a self-watering pot; it will stall the capillary action.

• Fertilizing a self-watering plant by normal means can be tricky. Instead, each time you top up the reservoir, use a solution of water and soluble fertilizer diluted to one quarter of the recommended strength.

• Leach the potting mix three or four times a year to remove accumulated fertilizer salts: Take the unit to the sink, remove the reservoir, and run tepid water through the soil mix until the drainage water runs perfectly clear.

• Since plants grown in self-watering pots produce fewer roots than plants grown in ordinary pots, they will not need to be repotted as frequently.

• If your system works well for a while, then the soil suddenly remains dry no matter how much water is in the reservoir, it is time to change the wick. Wicks eventually become clogged with mineral salts and no longer work efficiently.

MOVING PLANTS INDOORS AND OUT

After a long, dark winter, many houseplants enjoy a dose of fresh air, filtered sunlight, and rainwater. This treatment rejuvenates them and adds a fresh touch of greenery to porch, patio, or yard. However, it is not highly recommended for plants that you do not want to grow any larger or more vigorously, and it does require care and planning.

Take only the hardiest plants outdoors, those that will stand unexpected wind and cold. Always wait until all threat of frost has passed and temperatures are remaining above 45° F at night. Make the transition gradually, starting the plants out with at least a week in a protected, well-shaded spot. After a few weeks, you can settle most plants in a spot where there are a few hours of filtered sunlight each day and protection from the wind. Never place the plant in full sun. During the first few weeks, keep a close watch for evidence of excessive dryness, pest infestation, or shock.

You can display the plants outdoors in their containers or sink the pots below ground level in the garden, provided the site has good drainage. Dig a bed 3 or 4 inches deeper than the pots and wide enough to accommodate the foliage without it overlapping. Layer the bottom of the bed with 3 inches of gravel and 1 inch of peat moss. Set the pots into the bed and fill with soil up to the rims. The gravel should prevent the roots from spreading out of the drainage holes, but you may want to make sure they don't root into the ground by twisting the pots every few weeks.

As temperatures begin to dip in autumn, prepare to bring the plants back indoors. Set each container on a bench or table where you can examine it carefully, and clip off every yellowed leaf, spent flower, and seedpod. If the

Hydroculture

Hydroculture is one step beyond the self-watering pot. This technique uses no soil or organic material of any kind as a support. The plants grow entirely in stones or, more frequently, clay pebbles. Hydroculture reduces the danger of soil pests and diseases while supplying the plant with exactly the amount of water it needs. It is the ideal technique for people who don't have time to baby their plants, because the plants need watering only every two to three weeks. And those people who are allergic to plants (they are generally allergic to soil-borne organisms) may find that with hydroculture they can now enjoy houseplants as a hobby. Virtually any houseplant—even cacti and succulents—will adapt to hydroculture.

Hydroculture simply means growing in water. It is a simplified or passive version of another technique, hydroponics. In hydroponic systems, water is recirculated on a regular basis using pumps or other mechanical means. Hydroculture systems consist of an outer pot that serves as a reservoir for a liquid nutrient solution and a grow pot filled with clay pebbles, with a screen between the two pots. In hydroculture systems, water simply moves from one clay pebble to the next by capillary action, much as water moves in a self-watering pot. The texture of the pebbles allows plentiful air circulation, necessary for healthy root growth, while giving the roots all the moisture they require. There are no circulating pumps or bothersome tubes.

Before transferring plants to a hydroculture pot, rinse them thoroughly to remove any soil particles. Also, trim off any dead or dying roots;

otherwise rot can result. To make the transition to the new medium easier for the plants, mist them daily for the first 10 days after transplanting.

In many cases, rather than transplanting soil-grown plants, it is easier to start with new cuttings rooted in the hydroculture pot using special rooting stones, actually small versions of the regular clay pebbles. Transfer the cuttings to their final hydroculture pot once they have rooted. Some merchants stock plants raised in a hydroculture unit, making it easy to get started.

Using hydroculture pots is simple. You need to add water only when there is none left in the outer pot. In most cases, this means waiting until the indicator reads empty, then delaying two more days. To check that the container is empty, tip it and note whether the indicator moves. Then add enough water to bring the indicator up to the halfway mark. If you fill the pots to the top each time, the roots may rot. Use the maximum capacity of the container only when you will be away for several weeks. Leach the plants every two to three months, being sure to use room-temperature or tepid water.

Since there is no soil to buffer pH levels and mineral concentrations in the water, it is important to use fertilizers especially formulated for hydroculture. Some liquid and soluble hydroculture fertilizers are designed to be added each time the container is filled with water. Others are slow-release fertilizers, usually in the form of crystals or disks. They should be applied according to label instructions, which is usually once every six months.

Many hardy houseplants benefit from a summer spent in the fresh air and filtered sunlight of an outdoor location.

plant has grown too large for its indoor location, reshape it with some careful pruning.

Before bringing the plant inside, clean both the plant and the outside of the pot. Carefully examine the foliage for pests and disease, since these might infect your other plants. Treat pest-infested plants with the appropriate control, following the directions on the label. Once they are back inside, the plants will need to be acclimated (see page 35) just as they were when you first bought them.

You can also bring outdoor plants inside. If a certain potted plant is in full bloom, why not bring it inside so you can enjoy it? Before you move it, though, clean the plant and pot thoroughly, checking for insects and disease. Then

place the plant at the chosen site, and check to be sure it has sufficient water and light. After the blooms have faded, return it to its outdoor location. For more information on bringing plants indoors, see pages 96 and 97.

CREATING TERRARIUM GARDENS

Terrariums are miniature landscapes, created by combining a collection of plants in a glass container. The container can be made from a fish tank, bubble bowl, brandy snifter, or bottle. Depending on the choice of plants, the location, and the type of container, you can create the effect of a woodland dell, a desert, a rocky coastline, or a tiny jungle.

Terrariums are usually thought of as table-top decorations, but they can also be suspended from ceiling hooks or wall brackets. If there is space in the terrarium, you can even add a shallow container of water to serve as a pond in the midst of the landscape.

Plants do best under clear glass, rather than tinted glass. Bowls, dishes, brandy snifters, and fish tanks are easy to plant and maintain because you can easily reach inside them with your hands.

Planting Terrariums

Thoroughly clean and dry the chosen container before you start planting. Before you add any plant to a bottle garden or terrarium, inspect it carefully for insects, diseases, and rotted roots. These problems are especially contagious under glass.

Most containers used for terrarium gardening have no drainage holes. To keep the growing medium sweet smelling and healthy, line the bottom of the container with ½ inch of charcoal chips (available where indoor plants are sold). Then add at least 1½ inches of potting mix. The best soils for terrariums are the soilless mixtures or commercially prepared growing media with a little extra vermiculite or perlite added to improve air circulation to the roots.

Small-necked bottles are quite a challenge, requiring delicate, long-handled tools. To place the growing medium in such a bottle, fashion a funnel from a rolled-up piece of newspaper. To move the soil around and shape the terrain, use a spade fashioned from a slender, wooden stake (a chopstick or bamboo skewer) with a small measuring spoon taped to the end. When you are ready to "bottle" the plants, gently remove most of the potting mix from the roots, drop each plant through the neck of the bottle, coax it into the right position with the "spade," and cover the roots with growing media.

Once the plants are in place, a final mulch or ground carpet of moss will complete the scene. Mist with clear water to settle the roots and to remove soil particles from the leaves as well as from the sides of the bottle.

Maintaining Terrariums

The most common misconception about terrarium plantings is that they require no care and will thrive just about anywhere indoors. In fact, they need occasional watering and regular

grooming to remove spent growth and to contain fast-growing plants. Buying a preplanted terrarium stuffed with plants is not a good investment, as it will soon be overgrown.

Terrariums do best in bright indirect light—sunlight shining directly through the glass for more than an hour or two is likely to cook the plants. Terrariums also do well under two 20- or 40-watt fluorescent tubes—one cool white, one warm white for 12 to 14 hours a day.

When the soil appears dry, there are no moisture droplets on the container, or the plants are droopy, add a little water. To remove yellowing leaves, spent flowers, or excess growth from a narrow-necked bottle garden, tape a single-edge razor blade to a thin, wooden stick and use it as a cutting tool. You can remove the clippings with slender pieces of wood, manipulating them like chopsticks (slender, pointed, Japanese-style chopsticks will serve very well). You can also use a mechanic's pick-up tool (sold at auto supply stores). Remove dying leaves and flowers before they rot, since a tiny amount of rot can quickly infect healthy leaves and shoots.

Resembling a miniature greenhouse, this terrarium would lend a touch of greenery to any setting.

Propagating Techniques

Propagating new plants, whether by seed, cuttings, division, or layering, adds an entirely new dimension to the enjoyment of growing houseplants.

Collecting plants is no different from collecting anything else—increased knowledge tends to lead to rarefied tastes and inevitably higher prices. So once you're hooked, indoor gardening can be an expensive hobby. Propagation—the creation of new plants from old plants—is one of the most rewarding, easy, and economical ways to support your plant-growing habit. Propagating new plants also intimately involves you in the entire cycle of plant growth.

Starting new plants from old ones offers several benefits. You can multiply a few plants into a sizable collection or grow a beautifully symmetrical replacement for an aging favorite specimen. You can reproduce favorites from friends' collections with cuttings. And you can repay those same friends with gifts reproduced from plants in your collection. All you need is the knowledge of the correct techniques, a minimal investment in propagating materials, a little time and effort, and the patience to wait for a cutting to reach maturity.

On the following pages you will find discussions on how to germinate seeds and propagate from stem, leaf, and root cuttings as well as how to divide plants, separate and root plantlets, perform layering, and grow ferns from spores. The best propagation method to use depends on both the plant and your personal preference. Check with a houseplant specialist for the recommended propagation method for a specific plant.

Creating new plants from existing specimens helps you add to your plant collection.

Planting seeds is usually the least expensive way of starting new plants. There is a certain excitement in watching a seedling push through the soil, straighten up, and begin to grow.

PLANT PROPAGATION

Plants propagate in two fundamentally different ways—sexually and asexually. Sexual propagation occurs when pollen from the male parts of the plant fertilizes the female parts to produce seeds. Asexual propagation, or vegetative propagation, occurs when a piece of one plant is cultivated and grown into a new plant. The new plant is simply an extension of the original parent plant.

SEEDS

A seed is a tiny plant waiting for the right conditions to propel it into its life cycle. For germination it needs a disease-free growing medium, proper warmth and moisture, and adequate light. Propagating from seed allows you to enjoy species not normally available, acquire a number of plants of the same species cheaply, explore genetic variability, and gain a more intimate knowledge of a species.

Most houseplants may be grown from seed, but usually they are easier to propagate vegetatively. Several popular houseplants, however, can be propagated only from seed. Single-trunk palms, cyclamen, and many annuals used in hanging baskets fall in this category, as do the herbs parsley, chervil, sweet basil, marjoram, and summer savory. As an experiment try starting citrus plants from seeds that you've washed and allowed to dry. Lemon, lime, orange, and citron all make lovely houseplants, but you should not expect fruit from these plants. You can delight children by sowing a few dry peas or beans, or unroasted peanuts, all of which are seeds. Under the right conditions they will burst into growth.

Houseplant seeds are available from garden centers and a few mail-order nurseries. Sow them in the same way you would sow seed for outdoor plants, with bottom heat (70° to 75° F) to expedite germination (see pages 105 to 107).

For containers you can use flats, small pots, Styrofoam containers, cut-off milk cartons, or egg trays with small holes punched in the bottom with a needle. Small plastic or Styrofoam trays with clear plastic covers make excellent seed propagators as long as you make drainage holes.

Large seeds with hard coats should be nicked with a file and soaked in water until the coats soften, and then sown. Slow-germinating seeds (for instance, all species of the carrot family, including parsley and chervil) also benefit from a day or two of soaking.

An easy way to start seeds is to sow them in moistened vermiculite or milled sphagnum moss, both available at garden centers. Sow seeds sparingly so that the seedlings don't get crowded. Scatter tiny seeds on top of moist growing medium and leave them uncovered. Sow medium-sized seeds on the growing medium; cover them with a thin layer of the medium to hold them in place when they are watered. Cover large seeds to a depth twice their diameter, firming the growing medium around each seed by pressing gently.

Label the seed tray with the seed name, date sown, and any other information you may need. (It may also be useful to keep the seed packets so that you can refer to them for information on transplanting and suggested growing conditions.) Water lightly, and slip the seed tray into a plastic bag or cover it with paper or glass—the seed packet will indicate whether light or darkness is required for germination. Follow the directions and check seeds daily, watering when necessary. If you are growing tropical houseplants, be prepared to wait—some seeds take several years to germinate!

When seedlings emerge, move them into brighter light. The first two leaves to appear are generally not true leaves but cotyledons, which nourish the stem tip and the true leaves that follow. Wait for true leaves to appear before placing the seedlings in direct sunlight; then give them the same light you would give the mature plant. When the seedlings are three to four weeks old, start to fertilize them every two weeks with a diluted solution of liquid fertilizer (one third to one quarter the regular strength).

Transplant seedlings when they have at least four true leaves. Pry them out carefully, and place them into individual small pots filled with an appropriate potting mix.

If you decide to try to propagate one of the more challenging plants from seed, learn its needs first. Many specialty seed sources will tell you what they are, as will horticulture reference texts and local plant societies. Be sure you know whether you should cover the seed or sow it on the surface, since some seeds need light to germinate. Learn how long you can expect to wait for germination. Some species can take months to show.

Finally, see if the seeds must be treated before they will germinate. Some require stratification, which is cold treatment in the refrigerator for six weeks or longer at 35° to 40° F. Other seeds have a coat so tough that it must be broken before the seed can germinate. This treatment, called scarification, is achieved by nicking the seed coat with a file or sandpaper.

Houseplants to Grow From Seed

Botanical Name	Common Name
Agapanthus	Agapanthus, blue African lily, lily-of-the-Nile
Aglaonema modestum	Chinese evergreen
Asparagus	Asparagus fern
Begonia × *semperflorens-cultorum*	Wax begonia
Bromeliaceae	Bromeliads
Browallia	Browallia, sapphire-flower
Cactaceae	Cacti
Campanula	Star-of-Bethlehem, bellflower
Carissa macrocarpa	Ornamental pepper
Citrus species	Citrus
Coffea arabica	Coffee plant
Coleus × *hybridus*	Coleus
Crossandra infundibuliformis	Crossandra, firecracker-flower
Cuphea ignea	Cigar plant
Cyclamen persicum	Cyclamen
Exacum affine	Persian violet
Felicia amelloides	Blue marguerite, blue daisy
Gesneriaceae	Gesneriads
Hypoestes phyllostachya	Hypoestes, pink-polka-dot, freckle-face
Impatiens species	Impatiens
Palmae	Palms
Pelargonium	Florist's geraniums
Peperomia species	Peperomia
Persea americana	Avocado
Primula	Primrose
Thunbergia alata	Black-eyed-susan, thunbergia

CUTTINGS

Inducing a cutting to form roots is the most popular method of vegetative propagation. It is an easy way to duplicate the attractive features of the original plant, since the new plant will be genetically identical to the original. The new plant is in fact called a clone.

Depending on the plant, you can take cuttings from stems, leaves, and roots. Cuttings will root in a number of different media: in a commercial rooting medium, in water, in an artificial soil mix, or in potting mix. You will want to work quickly, so prepare the rooting medium and container before you take the cutting from the plant.

Although some gardeners routinely dip all cuttings in powdered rooting hormone before rooting them, this step is not usually necessary and may actually inhibit fast-rooting plants, such as coleus and Swedish ivy (*Plectranthus*). Plants with slightly woody stems, such as fuchsia and miniature rose, are more likely to benefit from use of a rooting hormone.

Stem Cuttings

With a very sharp knife or a razor blade, remove a leafy stem that is 1 to 6 inches long. Cut at an angle just below a node—the joint from which the leaf stalk arises—and trim the base with a clean cut about ⅛ of an inch above the lowest leaf node. Make sure the cutting has at least one node.

Strip off all but the top two or three sets of leaves. If the leaves are small and bunched together, you may leave a few more; if the leaves are large, retain only the last two and cut them in half width-wise with scissors. Try to leave about 2 square inches of leaf surface on each cutting—this may be several small leaves or only a part of one large one. Set the stripped end of the cutting in the rooting medium; then pat the soil around it so it is firmly in place.

When taking a stem cutting from a plant with a milky stem, such as poinsettia (*Euphoria pulcherrima*) or geranium (*Pelargonium*), make the cut, and then rub the cut end with alcohol (to prevent disease) and allow it to dry or callus for a few hours out of the sun. When the cut end is dry, proceed with planting the cutting in the rooting medium.

Leaf Cuttings

Some plants have the amazing ability to reproduce from a single leaf. The African violet (*Saintpaulia*) is well known for this characteristic, but this technique works equally well

Top: Herbaceous plants are easy to propagate from stem cuttings. Take cuttings using a sharp knife, as shown with this geranium (Pelargonium). Center: Remove the lower leaves as well as excessive top growth. Bottom left: With a pencil, make a hole in a moistened soilless growing medium and insert the trimmed cutting into the hole. Bottom right: Cover the cutting with a plastic cup or a staked plastic bag. Remove the plastic cover after a few days.

for florist's gloxinias (*Sinningia speciosa*), rex begonias, sedums, kalanchoes, and even some succulents and peperomias.

Certain species produce new plants from only a section of a leaf, providing the section contains a piece of midrib. Cape primrose (*Streptocarpus*) and a few other plants can be propagated by simply laying leaf sections on top of the rooting medium. Leaf sections of the snakeplant (*Sansevieria trifasciata*) will root and grow if the base is inserted just below the surface of the rooting medium.

To start a plant from a leaf cutting, pull or cut a mature, but not obviously old, leaf away from the parent plant. Cut the leaf stem (petiole) to ½ to 1 inch in length; set the leaf in the rooting medium as you would a stem cutting. The leaf should be at a 45-degree angle to the rooting medium (it can rest against the pot edge), and the cut end should not be placed too deep in the medium. Once plantlets form, cut away the parent leaf and transplant the new plantlets.

Root Cuttings

Some plants can be propagated from latent buds in their roots. Although relatively few houseplants are propagated this way, they include the edible fig (*Ficus carica*) and the Hawaiian ti plant (*Cordyline terminalis*).

To propagate from a root cutting, simply set the root pieces vertically in rooting medium. The ends that were closest to the crown should be at the top. When plantlets form, transplant them as you would other types of cuttings that have rooted.

Rooting Stem, Leaf, and Root Cuttings

Cuttings often fail to root because they dry out before being planted. To avoid disappointment, choose a work area out of direct sunlight and have the container and rooting medium at hand before you take the cutting. After you've severed it from the mother plant, root it quickly. The exception is leaf cuttings from a plant with milky sap, which need to dry and form a callus before rooting.

Various media are suitable for rooting cuttings. Whichever you choose, it should be light and porous, able to hold plenty of water, and coarse enough to allow air to circulate through it. It should also be sterilized. Never use a soil-based mix as a rooting medium; it is too rich for the immature roots of cuttings. One of the best rooting media is a mixture of 1 part sand and

Top left: Some plants can be propagated from a single leaf. Use a broken leaf or cut one off the parent plant.
Top right: Make a diagonal cut at the base of the stem with a sharp knife, as shown here.
Bottom: Place the cutting in a moistened growing medium and cover it with plastic for a few days.

1 part sphagnum peat moss. You can also use straight vermiculite, perlite, or milled sphagnum moss, or a mixture of 10 parts perlite to 1 part peat moss. Once you've made your choice, wet the rooting medium and let it drain.

You can start a plant in almost any container that will hold the rooting medium. People have successfully propagated plants in egg cartons, cut-off milk cartons, aluminum foil pans, tin cans, and plastic containers. Plastic pots are preferable to clay pots because they retain moisture longer. Commercial flats and pots are also available.

A clear plastic box makes an excellent propagator for multiple cuttings. Use a heated ice pick or awl to punch a few ventilation holes in the lid, lay about 2 inches of rooting medium on the bottom, moisten it, and the box is ready for the cuttings. A similar propagating box can be made from a seed flat or fruit box, covered by a sheet of glass or polyethylene film.

Clean any container thoroughly with soap and water before rooting the cuttings. Cuttings rooted in new wood-and-fiber flats or in paper containers will need extra nitrogen; some flats have extra fertilizer incorporated into them, or you can add fertilizer (see pages 50 to 52). Cuttings rooted in nonporous containers do better with drainage holes.

Use your index finger or a pencil to make a hole in the rooting medium, insert the cutting, and tamp soil around it until it is firmly in place. Cover the container with glass or plastic (making sure that it doesn't touch the foliage) and set it in a warm, light place with no direct sunlight. Since the cuttings initially have no roots and therefore can't supply the leaves with water, they must not dry out. You may need to water once or twice a day to keep the soil wet if you don't use a glass or plastic cover.

However, be careful not to waterlog the growing medium. Rooting boxes frequently don't have drainage holes, so overwatering will lead to root rot. If you are using a plastic bag or glass cover, be sure to open the bag or remove the cover for a few hours every day to allow fresh air to circulate.

Another popular method of rooting cuttings is to place them in a glass of water until roots have formed and then transplant them into a soilless mix. Rooting will occur more quickly if you place each cutting in a separate glass. Do not delay transplanting, since cuttings left too long in water will develop roots that have adapted to growing underwater. These roots may rot when they come into contact with a drier medium. Transplant as soon as roots are clearly visible but no longer than 1 inch long.

Several plant species can be grown permanently in water if fed frequently with liquid plant food. Wandering-Jew (*Tradescantia* or *Zebrina* species), arrowhead vine (*Syngonium podophyllum*), and philodendrons can easily be grown this way (see the discussion of hydroculture on page 61). Keep in mind that plants growing in water are more susceptible to rot than those in a rooting medium.

Many flowering and foliage plants, such as columneas and begonias, root so easily that you can place the cuttings directly in the final containers. Given reasonable humidity, a porous soil mix, and ample water from the start, the cuttings will root in weeks and produce mature container plants in one season.

Bottom heat   Nearly all cuttings benefit from the addition of bottom heat. They will root particularly quickly if you keep the tops of the cuttings cool (55° to 65° F) and the bottom of the containers warm (70° to 75° F). Experiment with different locations to find the one that works best for cuttings. Many gardeners have had success by placing flats on top of the refrigerator or on a gas dryer in the laundry room (the pilot light provides bottom heat).

Inexpensive soil-heating cables are available in various sizes at many garden supply centers. Personnel there can often help you choose the most suitable unit for your needs. If you intend to root cuttings regularly, consider constructing a bottom-heated bench (see page 107). If you install a heating source, adjustable ventilation, and automatic misting, you will be able to leave cuttings unattended for a few days with no harm done.

Problems   Rot is the most common problem in rooting cuttings. Try to maintain a healthy environment by renewing the rooting medium in a rooting bench with fresh materials every six months if it's in continual use and by removing any fallen leaves and rotted stems promptly. If the mix is constantly wet, try using pure perlite. If it dries out too quickly, add fine peat moss in the proportion of 1/10 to 1/5 of the total mix.

Opposite, top: Bromeliads can be propagated by dividing offsets from the parent plants. Slice through the soil with a sharp knife, making sure you take some of the basal growth and roots. Opposite, bottom: Pot the division in its own container and provide it with the same growing conditions as for the parent plant.

Timing also affects the rooting of cuttings. Many species simply won't root in winter. Some cuttings root only when taken from new shoots (softwood cuttings). If a cutting fails to root, or if the new plant dies, try again with a new cutting a few weeks later.

Transplanting Cuttings

Rooting takes from one to six weeks or more, depending on the plant. You can tell that roots have begun to grow when the foliage perks up and the plant puts out new growth. You can test by tugging gently on the cutting; if it doesn't pull out of the soil readily, you will know it has rooted.

Remove the plastic or glass cover once the cutting has rooted, at first for an hour or two daily and then for several hours. Then discard the cover and move the plant to a permanent container.

The best way to determine when the plant is ready to be transplanted is by gently lifting it out of the rooting medium and observing the root length. The roots should not be more than an inch long when you transplant; otherwise, they may tear off.

Move new plants out of the sterile rooting medium and into the permanent growing medium as soon as possible, since rooting media hold no nutrients to feed the plants. Be sure the container is the right size and not too large for the young plant (see page 54).

DIVISIONS

Some houseplants are easier to propagate by dividing the entire plant, including the root system and foliage, into two or more smaller plants. A plant that forms new plant clusters at its base or whose stems emerge from its base is best propagated by division. Some examples are the cast-iron plant (*Aspidistra elatior*), papyrus (*Cyperus papyrus*), ferns, and many begonias, prayer-plants (*Maranta*), and such cluster-forming succulents as certain sedums and jade plants (*Crassula argentea*). Foliage plants should be divided in early spring, when the plants are just beginning to produce new growth. Flowering plants are best divided during their dormant period.

Division is not a delicate technique. Remove the plant from its container, and slice down through the rootball with a sharp knife or sharpened spade. You may need to saw some plants apart, but others you can gently break apart by hand. (Don't worry about damaging the plants or treating the cuts. Once you've taken the divisions, just replant or repot the parent.)

Each division should include some of the main root and stem system. Plant the divisions immediately in permanent containers with potting soil, and water thoroughly. Keep them in bright light but out of direct sun, watering frequently until they root. It may also be helpful to place the divisions inside a clear plastic bag in order to reduce moisture loss. When they appear upright and healthy, place them in a permanent location and care for them as you would mature plants.

Offsets

Offsets are small, new plants that form at the base of the old plant and remain attached to it. They can be broken off and planted to form new plants, just like divisions.

Many succulents and bromeliads produce offsets from dormant buds on the main stem, near ground level. The offsets sometimes completely surround the parent plant and are ready to take over when it dies. Remove them by cutting them off close to the main stem; then place them in an appropriate rooting environment. For most succulents and bromeliads, this means setting the offsets in slightly smaller pots amid pieces of fir bark.

Detach offsets only when they are mature enough to survive on their own—usually when they have taken on the look of the mature plant. If you provide the temperature and light conditions that the plant prefers, new roots will form quickly. The screwpine (*Pandanus veitchii*), a foolproof houseplant, can be propagated this way.

Plantlets

Several common houseplants, such as the spiderplant (*Chlorophytum*), flame-violet (*Episcia*), and many species of Boston fern

Water the cup formed by the bromeliad leaves and, very infrequently, moisten the roots.

(*Nephrolepis exaltata*), reproduce by sending out miniature new plants on runners or shoots. When they begin to form aerial roots, the plantlets can be separated from the parent.

Root a plantlet by filling a small pot with moist rooting medium and placing it alongside the parent plant. Without severing the runner, lay the plantlet on top of the soil in the new pot and hold it in place with a hairpin or piece of wire. Keep the soil moist. New growth on the plantlet signals that it has rooted. It can now be severed from the parent.

Alternatively, clip off the runner and insert the base of the plantlet into a moist propagating medium. Cover with glass or plastic film until the new roots form.

It is not always necessary to remove a plantlet to get it to root. Plantlets formed on the runners or shoots of the spiderplant (Chlorophytum comosum) or the piggyback plant (Tolmiea menziesii) can be pinned into the moist soil in the same pot as the parent.

Leave the plantlets growing alongside the parent plant until they are rooted.

Unlike most plants that propagate by runners, the piggyback plant (*Tolmiea menziesii*) forms plantlets on top of its mature leaves. However, you can root them in the same manner as you would plantlets on runners.

Bulbs

Many bulbous plants, such as amaryllis (*Hippeastrum*), can be propagated by dividing their tuberous roots, tubers, or rhizomes or by separating new corms and bulbs from the original plant. In some cases, such as tulips (*Tulipa*), the old bulb disappears, leaving behind one or more offspring. After flowering, the foliage of most bulbous plants continues to grow, creating food reserves in the bulbs and bulblets for the next season. The foliage then begins to yellow as the plants enter their dormant period. When this happens, withhold water until all the foliage has died back. Then take the plant out of the container and divide the bulb or separate any small bulblets that have formed beside the parent bulb. It may take several years for a plant started from a bulblet to become large enough to produce a flower.

Bulbs of the scaly type can be propagated by peeling off one or two layers of scales and laying the scales on rooting medium. Easter lilies (*Lilium longiflorum*) reproduce this way. Dust the scales with fungicide and a rooting powder, and seal them in a plastic bag filled with damp vermiculite. Keep the bag at room temperature until bulblets form—about two months—and then cool them in the refrigerator for another two months before planting.

Plants that form from tubers, such as gloxinia, tuberous begonia, and caladium, can be propagated by division. After the eyes, or buds, have begun to swell in spring, cut the tuber into pieces, making sure each piece has a bud. Dust each piece with fungicide and plant just beneath the surface of a moist rooting medium.

Corms, Rhizomes, and Tubers

Houseplants grown from corms, rhizomes, and tubers have a thickened stem or root, modified for food storage, from which leaves and flowers grow. Timing is important in propagating these plants. If they have a dormant period, propagate when the plant is about to send up new green shoots.

Tuber division works for large specimens of florist's gloxinia (*Sinningia speciosa*), tuberous begonia (*Begonia* × *tuberhybrida*), and caladium. After the eyes, or buds, on the tubers have begun to swell in spring and are clearly visible, simply cut the tuber into pieces, being sure that every section has a bud. Dust the cut surfaces with a fungicide, and plant each piece just below the surface in a moist rooting medium. Provide good air movement to reduce the chance of fungus or bacterial rot; if you see rot beginning, cut off the infected surface and start over.

The lovely glory lily (*Gloriosa rothschildiana*) produces cigar-shaped tubers that can be broken into pieces and replanted. Ferns that form rhizomes can also be cut into pieces and replanted.

Theoretically, plants with corms, such as freesias, can be divided, but getting a bud in each division is tricky. It is easiest to replant the many small new corms, called cormels, that form around the parent corm. Separate them and replant them about 2 inches deep.

LAYERING

Propagation by layering is similar to rooting cuttings, except that the part of the plant (usually a branch) to be rooted remains attached to the parent plant. The great advantage of layering is that the parent plant supplies the cutting with water and nutrients while the roots are forming. Daily maintenance of the cutting is therefore unnecessary.

To be suitable for layering, a plant needs to have a branch low enough that you can bend it into contact with the growing medium. If there is such a branch, bend it, make a notch at the point of contact with the mix, then bury that portion of the branch. Securely immobilize it with a peg, a broken hairpin, a paper clip that has been straightened and bent in the shape of a U, or a rock. A rock will also keep the soil beneath it moist.

To layer a plant without taking a cutting, bend a low branch so that it is in contact with the growing medium. Notch the point of contact on the branch and bury it beneath the surface of the growing medium.

Immobilize the rooting branch with a peg or rock. Be prepared to wait several months for root formation.

Layering is best done in spring. Root formation is likely to take several months. Spring is also the best time for detaching the rooted branch, so it may be best to leave the layer attached for a full year. When you are ready to detach the branch, lift the branch from the potting mix at the point where roots have formed, then cut it from the parent plant and treat it as a rooted cutting.

A number of low-growing species, such as the screwpine (*Pandanus*), will self-layer. Detach the rooted branch and transplant it in the same way.

Air-layering works well for some genera, such as dumb-cane (*Dieffenbachia*), flame-violet (*Episcia*), and pothos (*Epipremnum aureum*), that lack branches conveniently close to the ground. It is especially useful for salvaging

Top: To air-layer a plant, cut into, but not through, the stem with a sharp knife.
Center: Insert a wedge into the stem to keep the cut open.
Bottom: Cover the cut with damp moss and wrap it in plastic. When roots appear, cut off the stem and pot the rooted plant.

leggy plants or mature specimens that have lost their lower leaves.

With a sharp knife, make a shallow cut no more than halfway through a stem at about a foot from the growing tip. Insert a thin piece of wood (such as a matchstick) to hold the cut open. Wrap the stem with a handful of coarse, wet sphagnum moss or a damp sponge; cover with plastic wrap; and secure with tape or rubber bands above and below the cut. When new roots form in the moss, cut off the stem below the rooted section and pot the new plant. If months go by before rooting occurs, you may have to wet the moss by poking a small hole in the wrap and squirting water inside. If the stem fails to produce roots, try again: Open up the wrapping, nick the stem, dust the cut with rooting hormone, and retie.

FERN SPORES

Unlike most other plants, ferns produce tiny spores, not seeds, and are challenging to propagate. The spores are tiny, very slow to germinate and grow, and must be continually protected from dry air. If you want to try propagating ferns, you will need plenty of patience. Look on the undersides of the fronds for ripe spore cases and brush the spores into an envelope. Allow them to dry for a few weeks before trying to germinate them.

The brick-and-box method is perhaps the most effective way of germinating spores. Place a brick in a transparent plastic box and add 2 inches of water. Cover the top of the brick with ¼ inch of milled peat moss. Wet both the brick and the moss, and dust the fern spores on top of the moss; cover the box with glass or plastic to retain the moisture.

Place the box in a dimly lit spot with moderate temperatures (65° to 75° F), and leave it there for several months. Eventually, the germinated spores will produce a mossy mat on top of the covered brick. This is the sexual stage of the ferns. When the mat looks strong, break off 1-inch pieces and transplant them into a flat filled with an all-purpose potting mix. Keep the flat moist and covered for several more months or until small ferns appear. When the ferns are 2 to 3 inches high, transplant them to individual pots. Check the water level every few days while the spores are germinating, adding water when necessary to maintain the level at 2 inches.

Indoor Herb Gardens

Any cook appreciates the convenience of fresh herbs growing in the kitchen, and an indoor herb garden is also decorative. Even an apartment dweller with no outdoor garden space can produce an herb crop.

With the right growing conditions, a surprising number of plants can be successfully grown indoors. Most cooking herbs grow well in small to medium-sized pots. Clay or terra-cotta pots contrast well with herb foliage, but herbs will also grow in glazed pots, in a window box, or even, with proper care, in a hanging basket.

All herbs require a growing medium with good drainage; herbs with moisture-soaked roots won't flourish. Keep herbs out of the way of areas with abrupt temperature changes, such as by a stove. Finally, be sure the plants receive plenty of light. You may want to rotate the container with each watering to ensure even light and growth for the plants, especially if you are growing herbs in a hanging basket.

Your choice of plants should follow your culinary preferences. Favorites include basil, parsley, sage, and mint, but you might also try chives, chervil, dill, French tarragon, lemon thyme, and marjoram. Although rosemary and bay do best in individual pots, they'll grow indoors with proper care.

A kitchen window is an ideal growing spot for this indoor herb garden, providing plenty of light and easy access for the cook. The wire basket lined with moss holds golden sage, thyme, oregano, and chiles, while the clay pots contain silver thyme.

Flowering Houseplants

Houseplants bursting with blooms add the appeal of cut flowers to a room. In many cases, they also contribute graceful foliage color to the decor once the blooms have faded.

If you want to add color and pattern to your indoor garden, there are several foliage plants that fill the bill, but a flowering houseplant will bring a burst of joy to the most cheerless room. Like most good things in life, however, joy doesn't come without some effort. Yet your efforts will be rewarded when you watch the delicate flowers unfold, adding charm and a touch of spring to your home.

Though definitions of a flowering houseplant vary from person to person, for the purposes of this book a flowering houseplant is one that can be grown and trained into a size, shape, and form compatible with indoor spaces and the living habits of the occupants of those spaces. Flowering houseplants are further categorized by how they adapt or acclimate to indoor light intensities and temperatures. Some plants, with care, will do fine with indoor light; others will bloom only with special help from you. A few flowering houseplants are outdoor species that have been forced into bloom for indoor use.

This stately collection of dwarf anthurium (Anthurium scherzeranum), *air plant* (Tillandsia), *and a basket containing streptocarpus, gazmania, and ivy covers the top of this low coffee table with blooms.*

Reiger begonias
(Begonia × hiemalis)
will bloom the year
around in a suitable
environment.

ENCOURAGING PLANTS TO BLOOM

Flowering indoor plants are often divided into four categories, according to the way in which they flower. Not all flowering plants bloom continually; a few, in fact, will not bloom indoors at all unless they receive special care. Two other important considerations that affect how a plant will bloom are the plant's exposure to light, known as photoperiodism, and the plant's exposure to cool temperatures, known as vernalization.

Photoperiodism

A poinsettia (*Euphorbia pulcherrima*) grown indoors will not ordinarily bloom. The controlling factor is the *photoperiod,* the length of time during each day that the plant is exposed to light. A poinsettia is called a short-day plant because it needs a series of short days and long nights to begin budding.

The critical factor for short-day plants is actually the length of the night. Indoors, plants often receive light in the evening from electric bulbs, so a poinsettia will never bloom unless you give it special treatment to mimic the long, dark nights of autumn outdoors.

To initiate flower buds that will mature by Christmastime, in late September or early October place the plant in a closet or other dark area for 12 to 16 hours a night for at least two weeks (preferably six weeks). Be careful not to open the closet door during treatment, and seal any cracks under the door. The dark periods must be total and continuous; even a small amount of light may cause sparse budding or deformed flowers. After plant begins to flower, place it in a bright, indirectly lit south, east, or west window. Keep the plant evenly moist throughout this period.

The florist's chrysanthemum (*Chrysanthemum × morifolium*), another short-day plant, gets special treatment at the nursery. Chrysanthemums flower naturally only in fall or early winter, but plant producers bring them into bloom throughout the year by using black-cloth shading techniques to simulate the necessary long nights.

Few flowers are as sensitive to photoperiodism as poinsettias and chrysanthemums, although researchers have found that photoperiod adjustment encourages flower development in many species, such as begonias and many gesneriads, that do not absolutely require specific photoperiods. Long-day plants, such as tuberous begonias (*Begonia × tuberhybrida*), pocketbook-flower (*Calceolaria crenatifolia*), and cineraria (*Senecio × hybridus*), can be brought into bloom during fall and winter by providing light at night. Even short bursts of light in the middle of the night may be enough to stimulate flower formation.

Vernalization

Some plants, such as the hardy bulbs, need a cold winter to thrive. These plants can be brought into bloom by placing them in cool storage (45° F or below) for several weeks. This process of creating an artificial winter is known as vernalization.

Plants that normally lose their leaves in winter, such as hydrangeas and many bulbous plants, can be kept in cool storage for several months. The cooler the area and the longer the storage, the more quickly flowers will develop when the plants are returned to normal growing temperatures. Refrigerators can make appropriate cool storage areas if basements and garages are not cool enough, provided the temperature stays above 35° F to prevent frost damage.

Plants in cool storage need to be moist but not wet. Some plants need artificial light to prevent excessive leaf drop. Even those species that do not require cooling to produce flowers may be invigorated by vernalization. Often it results in healthier growth and in increased flower production.

Plants That Bloom Continually

Many African violets (*Saintpaulia*), begonias, and other plants grown indoors flower continually, often for many years. They are truly the best of the indoor flowering plants. These plants need optimum care in a stable setting.

Plants That Bloom Seasonally or Intermittently

A wider variety of plants, such as peace-lilies (*Spathiphyllum*), kalanchoe (*Kalanchoe blossfeldiana*), Christmas cactus (*Schlumbergera*), or geraniums (*Pelargonium*), flower seasonally or intermittently throughout the year. They are induced to flower through proper management of temperature, light intensity,

An azalea (Rhododendron) *is best used as an indoor plant only while it is in bloom.*

The Fragrant Garden

Flowers can add more than just color to a room. Some beautiful bloomers also add a pleasant perfume to the air.

Light is a key ingredient in unleashing the aroma of a bloom. The more light a plant receives, the stronger the perfume. As with all other plants, the proper horticultural care will also help bring out the best in a fragrant houseplant.

Jasmine is the traditional favorite for sweet-smelling flowers. And since the perfume of most jasmines is most powerful at night, many working people can appreciate their fragrance during the hours they are at home. Almost all species of jasmine are fragrant, though not all perform equally well indoors. Two reliable choices are the poet's jasmine (*Jasminum grandiflorum*) and the Confederate-jasmine (*Trachelospermum jasminoides*).

That southern garden favorite, the gardenia (*Gardenia gasminoides*), scents the air with a heady aroma reminiscent of a woman's perfume. The African gardenia (*Mitriostigma axillare*) is actually easier to grow indoors than the common gardenia. Keep the air around it humid.

The tender narcissus 'Paper White' is another popular, and heady, aromatic plant. Most often forced for indoor bloom, paper-whites add the look and smell of spring to a winter-encircled home. Be aware that the aroma can be overwhelming in a small room.

Hyacinths (*Hyacinthus orientalis*), an old-fashioned favorite, bloom in late winter, filling a room with the aroma and promise of spring. The fragrant blossoms are red, pink, blue, yellow, or white. Purchase hyacinths in bloom from florists, or force your own bulbs from bulbs planted in October.

Citrus blossoms are known for their fresh, clean fragrance. A good choice for indoor gardens is × *Citrofortunella mitis*, a cross between a mandarin orange and a kumquat. With proper care, you can even get fruit for your efforts. It will probably be too bitter to eat fresh from the plant, but you can use it for cooking. Another plant with a similar fragrance is the orange-jasmine (*Murraya paniculata*), with its small, white flowers that combine the aromas of jasmine and orange blossoms.

light quality, day length (or night length), and pruning practices. Their usefulness in indoor gardens rests on their attractiveness as foliage plants as well as flowering plants. These plants are often moved about the home, depending on whether they are in flower. However, they shouldn't be neglected once they're out of the limelight; to encourage bloom, flowering plants need proper care the year around.

Plants That Need a Rest Period

Some of the indoor flowering plants that bloom seasonally or intermittently require a rest period (generally after they flower). Florist's gloxinia (*Sinningia speciosa*) is the most widely known plant in this category. It goes completely dormant, the foliage dies back, and the tuber is usually removed and stored in

Lilies (Lilium) *add color to a room while they are in bloom, but they are among the flowering houseplants that need a rest period after blooming.*

moist sphagnum moss until the next year. Other plants, such as most clerodendrons, become semidormant; they keep their foliage but do not produce any new growth during the rest period.

Bulbous plants forced indoors fall into this group of plants. Although some bulbous plants have adapted to years of indoor culture, most wither and go dormant after flowering. Many indoor gardeners use bulbs as a room decoration during their blooming period and then remove them to an out-of-the-way growing station when they start to die back.

Outdoor Plants That Bloom Indoors

Many flowering houseplants are houseplants only while they are in flower. The most popular flowering houseplants are in this category: Tulips, narcissus, chrysanthemums (*Chrysanthemum × morifolium*), and Easter lilies (*Lilium longiflorum*) all create a decorative accent indoors while they are in bloom. Afterward, they are either discarded, as is the case with most poinsettias (*Euphorbia pulcherrima*), chrysanthemums, and cinerarias (*Senecio ×*

hybridus), or moved to a greenhouse, window box, or outdoor flower bed.

Prolonging the Flowering Period

Your primary object in caring for your plants while they are flowering is to prolong the flowering period for as long as possible. With proper care, you can double the usual life of blooming plants in a decorative indoor setting.

Most plants that have been properly grown before they start to flower will have enough nutrients to carry them through the blooming period. Additional fertilization, especially without thorough watering, may actually damage the roots of plants in bloom.

Never allow the rootball to dry out. The soilless growing media that many commercial growers use is especially difficult to wet once it dries out. Excessive drying and root damage causes many plants to drop their leaves or buds.

Finally, keep blooming plants out of direct sunlight or drafts of hot, dry air. Petals cannot replenish lost moisture as easily as can leaves and may quickly burn, fade, or wilt.

Baskets, Reiger begonias (Begonia × hiemalis), and wax fruit form a three-dimensional still life on this kitchen shelf.

Dealing With Reluctant Bloomers

At some point you may find you have a plant that will not bloom. There are many possible causes for this, but the most common one is insufficient light.

Try giving the plant progressively more light. If it is not close to a light source, move it closer to the window or to lights. A drastic change in light intensity may burn the foliage, so make the change gradually. Don't be alarmed if the move bleaches the foliage a little. Unless the leaves turn yellow, the plant will not be damaged. Since placing a plant closer to a light source will cause it to dry out faster, keep a careful eye on it so that you can adjust to its new watering needs.

If a plant will not bloom under good light, it may need a change in day length. If the plant is usually in light for 12 hours each day, try a day length of 10 hours for a few weeks and then go back to 12 hours. If this does not work, try a few weeks at 14 hours of light a day (watch carefully to be sure this change does not create too much water stress).

Transplanting disrupts the growing routine and gives the roots more room, which inhibits flowering. Roots need time to grow into new growing medium. Instead of transplanting just before flowering, replace the top third of the soil with new mix until the blooming period is finished.

Many plants are simply too young to produce flowers. Often, woody plants must grow for a year or two before they will flower, and bulbous plants started from small bulbs will not flower for two or three years. Most of the newer cultivars of African violets (*Saintpaulia*) begin flowering when they are quite young, but this is not often the case with other species of plants.

Pruning and shaping enhance flower production, but only if there is enough foliage left for buds to form. Don't remove flower buds when pruning—pinch back the stems after the plant has bloomed.

It is important to remove the outer leaves of African violets to keep the plants flowering well. Unless they are removed, the inside rows will have no chance to produce flowers. Each row of leaves produces flowers only once. The third row of leaves, counting from the center outward, carries the mature blossoms. The new flower buds are produced in the center of the plant at the first row of leaves. Once a plant has more than five rows of leaves, the blossom number and size will gradually decline until the plant eventually stops flowering altogether.

The acidity of the potting mix is another factor that affects blooming. If the pH level is below 5 or over 8, the plant is unlikely to bloom. Furthermore, plants that are dormant can't be rushed into flowering.

Perhaps your reluctant bloomer just needs a rest. You can try withholding fertilizer and slightly reducing water for a month, then resume regular care. Sometimes flowering plants get into a rut and need a little contrived change of seasons or conditions to force them to develop flower buds. Experiment. You have nothing to lose, and you will learn from your experimentation. If everything you try fails, perhaps it's time to make room for a new plant in your collection.

Caring for Plants After Flowering

Unless you plan to discard the plant toward the end of its flowering period, you must change your care routine when it stops flowering. If you have distinct display and growing stations, this is most easily accomplished by returning the plant to its growing station. You can then place another flowering plant or a foliage plant in the display station.

Many plants require a rest immediately after flowering. Begin withholding water gradually over a period of a few weeks, and do not fertilize during this time. Withhold water by

Once a plant has bloomed, remove any spent blossoms and yellowing foliage and allow it to rest for a while.

watering less frequently, not by using less water at each irrigation. There's a temptation to cut back the foliage of bulbous plants once the flowers have faded. However, many bulbous plants need their foliage to produce food reserves for the next flowering cycle. Yellowing foliage naturally signals the onset of their dormancy; remove the foliage then.

To decorate a room successfully with flowering plants, it is important to discard or replace a plant once it is past its prime. Commercial interior landscapers call flowering plants "changeout plants" and refer to the process as "refreshing your garden"; they realize that they must keep rotating the plants to maintain a constantly decorative display.

It is easy to tell when a plant is past its flowering prime: The flowers are fading and no new buds are forming. It will not come back into bloom unless it is pruned and possibly repotted. Move the plant to a growing station and put a new specimen that has just begun to flower into the display station.

KEEPING POPULAR HOUSEPLANTS BLOOMING

Choices in flowering houseplants can be as varied as choices in decorating style. You'll find there's a perfect flowering plant for any home. Following is a list of some popular flowering plants for use indoors and some tips on keeping these plants in bloom.

Placing African violets (Saintpaulia) *near a mirror doubles the amount of color they bring to this hallway.*

This bougainvillea (Bougainvillea glabra) *trained as a topiary wreath and the low, spreading English ivy* (Hedera helix) *add color and repeat the delicate textures and patterns of this Victorian-inspired dressing table.*

African violet (*Saintpaulia*) Although it will bloom with 10 hours or less of light per day, long days will promote blooming. Leggy stems and the absence of blooms indicate insufficient light. Older varieties may bloom seasonally, with long rest periods between flowerings, but newer hybrids will often bloom nonstop the year around. Perfect for indoor culture because it thrives in night temperatures between 65° and 70° F. Blooms best when roots are crowded.

Begonia (*Begonia* species) *B.* × *hiemalis* and other winter-flowering types need a period of lower temperatures and long nights to set buds. Tuberous and fibrous begonias grow best during long days. However, tuberous types require long nights before they go dormant to set flower buds for the next year.

Blue daisy (*Felicia amelloides*) Pinch flowers off a young plant until it reaches the desired size. Warm temperatures and decreased watering increase blooming. Warm temperatures and bottom heat encourage rapid growth.

Bougainvillea (*Bougainvillea glabra*) Blooms best in strong light and high temperatures (70° to 80° F). Flowers form when day and night are of equal length. Plants do not like to be moved.

Bromeliad (numerous genera) Grows well with long days, but many, including the pineapple (*Ananas*), need long nights to set blooms. Keep warm and give plenty of light (60° F minimum at night, 75° F during the day).

Cacti (numerous genera) Need cool nights (45° to 50° F) to set flower buds. Watering after a long dry period also induces blooming. Cacti need strong light to flower well.

Calceolaria or pocketbook-flower (*Calceolaria crenatiflora*) Likes cool night temperatures (40° to 45° F) and day temperatures that are 15° higher. Growing plants to a large size is difficult. Flower buds need short nights to set.

Carnation (*Dianthus caryophyllus*) Blooms best after a period of short nights. Needs strong light to produce its fragrant flowers.

Chrysanthemum (*Chrysanthemum × morifolium*) Needs long, cool nights (45° to 50° F) to set buds, then warm temperatures to help buds develop into blooms; 13- to 14-hour nights also help bud set, providing the temperature remains below 68° F. The combination of warm temperatures and long nights prevents bud formation.

Cineraria (*Senecio × hybridus*) Difficult to force into bloom indoors. Needs cool nights, warm days, and good air circulation.

Citrus (*Citrus* species) Blooms best in strong light. Cool nights will encourage compact growth.

Clerodendrum or glorybower (*Clerodendrum thomsoniae*) Flowers only on new growth. After flowering, prune and then fertilize to promote new growth for next season.

Columnea (*Columnea* species) Grows well in long days. Needs cool nights (50° to 60° F) to promote flowering.

Cyclamen (*Cyclamen persicum*) Flowers like cool temperatures; 40° to 50° F at night is best. Goes dormant in summer and needs this resting period to bloom well.

Cymbidium (*Cymbidium*) Needs as much light as possible, but watch for burning. Dark green leaves indicate insufficient light. Will not bloom if nights are too warm; night temperatures of 50° to 55° F are best.

Episcia (*Episcia* species) Similar to African violet, but requires higher light intensities and more humidity to bloom well. Likes long days, crowded roots, and plenty of fertilizer. Keep air humid.

Flamingo-flower (*Anthurium*) Needs high humidity and high temperatures (80° to 90° F). Long days encourage blooming. Low humidity or low temperatures for even a few days may harm developing flowers.

Florist's azalea (*Rhododendron indica* varieties) Likes cool temperatures for growth, warmer temperatures for setting flower buds, and then cooler temperatures to mature the buds. Well-pruned, bushy plants will produce more blooms. Move outdoor plants indoors in October to bloom by December.

An exotic orchid and a humble geranium team up to add color to a hallway table.

Fuchsia (*Fuchsia* × *hybrida*) Needs cool temperatures (50° to 55° F at night, 68° to 72° F during the day). Must have high humidity to perform well. Long days encourage bud set.

Gardenia (*Gardenia jasminoides*) Needs long, cool nights (below 65° F) to set flower buds. Buds often drop if humidity is low, soil is too wet, or light is too low.

Geranium (*Pelargonium*) Zonal geraniums (*P.* × *hortorum*), with round leaf edge, bloom in strong light and warmth. Martha Washington geraniums (*P.* × *domesticum*), with jagged leaf edge, need 12- to 13-hour nights to set flower buds and then long days to develop buds into flowers.

Hibiscus (*Hibiscus rosa-sinensis*) Blooms best in long days and high humidity. Does not like to be moved. Prune heavily to keep bushy.

Hoya (*Hoya* species) Fragrant blooms form on stubby twigs. Blooms best in short nights. During winter, needs rest period of less light, water, and fertilizer.

Lovely and restrained, Persian violets (Exacum affine) *suit this formal setting.*

Hydrangea (*Hydrangea macrophylla*)
Needs a long, cool storage period and moist soil during dormancy to bloom again. Strong light and warmth promote flower development. Fertilize heavily to grow plants to good size. Splitting flower stems indicate too short a cooling period.

Impatiens or busy-lizzy (*Impatiens*)   Likes intermediate day length. New Guinea types develop best leaf color with long days, but bloom best in intermediate days (12 hours light, 12 hours dark).

Kalanchoe (*Kalanchoe blossfeldiana*)
Requires 6 weeks of long nights for flower bud formation. Blooms will begin 3 months after long nights begin.

Lantana (*Lantana*)   Likes high heat (75° to 85° F) and strong light. Will bloom indoors in winter if given short nights after being kept cool and shaded the previous summer.

Marigold (*Tagetes* species)   Grows best in 16-hour days; blooms best in 12- to 15-hour days. Give as much light as possible indoors.

The yellow flowers of a shrimp-plant (Justicia brandegeana) *and miniature primroses* (Primula) *evoke bright spring sunshine in any season.*

Nasturtium (*Tropaeolum majus*) Blooms best in long days. Needs cool nights (40° to 55° F) and day temperatures below 70° F.

Orchids (various genera) Most epiphytic (not grown in soil) orchids grow best in bright light. Need short days and cool nights (65° F or below) to set flower buds. Usually bloom in 4 months if growing conditions are right.

Peace-lily (*Spathiphyllum*) Mature healthy plants bloom best. Likes crowded roots and low-nitrogen soil. Plants kept too wet may grow well but fail to bloom.

Persian violet (*Exacum affine*) Needs short nights to bloom well. Growing plants to attain good size indoors is difficult. Give strong light and fertilize heavily.

These bulbs have been cooled in a cold frame and are ready for forcing. Having a cold frame is not essential because bulbs can be forced in a variety of containers.

Poinsettia (*Euphorbia pulcherrima*) Requires long nights for up to 6 weeks to form flower buds. Plants given long nights in late September through October will bloom by Christmastime. Bushy plants produce more blooms. Strong light and warmth (75° to 80° F) encourage larger plants and blooms.

Rose (*Rosa*) Grows best with long days and warm temperatures (60° to 65° F at night, 75° to 80° F during the day). Miniature roses do very well indoors. Increased light improves flower color. Miniatures can be kept in bloom for 8 to 9 months; then they require a rest period of 1 to 2 months. Night temperatures during the rest period should be approximately 40° F, and plants should be shaded.

Shrimp-plant (*Justicia brandegeana*) Blooms best with at least 4 hours of direct sunlight in winter and curtain-filtered sunlight from a south- or west-facing window in summer.

Snapdragon (*Antirrhinum majus*) Blooms best with short nights and cool temperatures. Dwarf varieties do well indoors any time of year. Seeds will germinate best if given a cooling treatment before sowing.

Tomato (*Lycopersicon lycopersicum*) Needs to dry out before flowers will form. Wet plants grow large but will not produce any fruit. Long days promote flower formation. Likes bottom heat when grown indoors out of season. Plants given excessive amounts of nitrogen may fail to bloom.

Zebra-plant (*Aphelandra squarrosa*) Blooms best at high temperatures (75° to 80° F); looks best when cut back to maintain bushiness. Long nights promote flower bud formation.

Zinnia (*Zinnia elegans*) Needs good air circulation and strong light to grow well indoors. Blooms best during long days. Dwarf varieties are easier to grow indoors.

FORCING BLOOMS INDOORS

Day length, light intensity, and temperature all change naturally in a seasonal cycle, bringing different plants into flower as the cycles change. Gardeners can imitate these changes to force flower development. Forcing is usually defined as an application of extra warmth to induce early flowering, but the full range of techniques is far greater.

Some plants are photoperiodic, which means that they will bloom only after they have been exposed to the correct ratio of light and dark periods during a day (see page 80). Other species may require a cool period that imitates winter. Some may not develop flowers, even if the day length is correct, unless the temperature is also correct.

Perhaps the most popular plants to force are bulbs. By duplicating—but shortening—the stages bulbs go through outdoors, you can have tulips, crocuses, daffodils, and hyacinths blooming indoors in the middle of winter. Other plants that can be easily forced include Dutch iris (*Iris xiphium* hybrids), grape hyacinth (*Muscari*), squill (*Scilla peruviana*), and ornithogalum. Several hardy perennials not normally grown as houseplants—hosta, astilbe, bleeding-heart (*Dicentra*), and lily-of-the-valley—can also be forced, along with annual flowers and branches of flowering shrubs.

Forcing Hardy Bulbs

Hardy bulbs are perhaps the most rewarding plants to force to bloom. Begin by buying the largest bulbs you can find. Select only those varieties clearly marked "good for forcing" (see chart at right for a list of bulb varieties for forcing). If you are buying by mail order, place your order as early as possible so that the bulbs will arrive in early fall. If you can't plant the bulbs immediately after their arrival, store them in opened bags or boxes in a cool place (35° to 55° F) or in the refrigerator, but for no more than a few weeks.

Plant bulbs around the beginning of October for flowers at Christmastime, in the middle of October for February flowers, and in November for March and April flowers. Bulbs can be forced in any number of containers, even ones without drainage holes. However, be sure the container is clean, and use a well-draining growing medium. If you are mixing your own, use equal parts soil, builders sand, and peat moss; to each 5-inch pot of the mix, add a teaspoon of bonemeal (see instructions for mixing your own growing medium on pages 46 to 48). You can also use an all-purpose potting mix with an added teaspoon of bonemeal.

Bulb Varieties for Forcing

Type	Color	Flowering Time
Crocuses		
'Flower Record'	Purple	Late winter, spring
'Joan of Arc'	White	Winter and spring
'Large yellow'	Yellow	Spring
'Peter Pan'	White	Winter and spring
'Pickwick'	Striped blue and white	Winter and spring
'Remembrance'	Purple	Winter and spring
'Victor Hugo'	Purple	Winter and spring
Daffodils (*Narcissus*)		
'Barrett Browning'	Orange cup, white perianth	Winter and spring
'Carlton'	Yellow	Winter
'Chinese Sacred Lily'	White	Winter and spring
'Dutch Master'	Yellow	Winter and spring
'Fortune'	Yellow and orange	Winter
'Ice Follies'	Cream cup, white perianth	Winter and spring
'Joseph MacLeod'	Yellow	Winter
'Magnet'	Yellow trumpet, white perianth	Spring
'Mt. Hood'	White	Winter and spring
'Paper White'	White	Winter and spring
'Soleil d'Or'	Yellow	Winter and spring
'Unsurpassable'	Yellow	Winter and spring
Grape hyacinth (*Muscari*)		
'Early Giant'	Blue	Winter and spring
Hyacinths (*Hyacinthus orientalis*)		
'Amethyst'	Violet	Spring
'Amsterdam'	Pink	Winter and spring
'Anne Marie'	Pink	Winter
'Bismarck'	Blue	Winter
'Blue Jacket'	Blue	Spring
'Carnegie'	White	Spring
'Colosseum'	White	Winter
'Delft Blue'	Blue	Winter
'Jan Bos'	Red	Winter
'Lady Derby'	Pink	Winter
'L'Innocence'	White	Winter
'Marconi'	Pink	Spring
'Marle'	Blue	Spring
'Ostara'	Blue	Winter and spring
'Pink Pearl'	Pink	Winter and spring
Irises		
'Harmony'	Blue	Winter and spring
'Hercules'	Purple	Winter and spring
Iris danfordiae	Yellow	Winter
Tulips (*Tulipa*)		
'Bellona'	Yellow	Winter
'Bing Crosby'	Red	Winter and spring
'Charles'	Red	Winter
'Christmas Marvel'	Pink	Winter
'Golden Eddy'	Red, with yellow or cream	Spring
'Hibernia'	White	Winter and spring
'Karel Doorman'	Red, with yellow or cream	Winter
'Kees Nelis'	Red, with yellow or cream	Winter
'Olaf'	Red	Winter and spring
'Ornament'	Yellow	Spring
'Paul Richter'	Red	Winter
'Peerless Pink'	Pink	Spring
'Preludium'	Pink	Winter
'Prominence'	Red	Late winter
'Stockholm'	Red	Winter
'Thule'	Yellow with red	Winter

Pot size depends on the type and quantity of bulbs you are forcing: One large daffodil or tulip bulb or three small crocuses will fill a 4- to 5-inch pot. Six tulips, daffodils, or hyacinths require an 8- to 10-inch pot. When planting several tulips in one pot, place the bulbs with the flat sides facing toward the outside of the pot so that the leaves will emerge facing outward.

Fill each pot loosely with soil mix. Place the bulbs in the pot so that their tops are just below the rim. Cover the tops of tulips, hyacinths, and small bulbs such as crocus with an inch of soil, but do not cover the necks and tops of daffodils. Avoid compressing the soil or pressing

the bulbs into it; the soil should remain loose so that roots can grow through it easily. After the bulbs are in, water the pots two or three times to moisten the soil and then let excess water drain. Label each pot as you plant it with the name of the flower and the planting date.

Most bulbs need a period of cool temperatures after potting and before forcing so that they can form a vigorous root system to support lush foliage and blooms. Without a potful of roots, bulbs will not bloom prolifically. Some bulbs have been precooled by the producer and can be planted and forced immediately. To prepare bulbs that have not been precooled, place

Daffodils (Narcissus) *forced to bloom bring the sunshine indoors on even the most dismal rainy winter day.*

them in a cool, frost-free place, such as an un-heated garage or basement, or an old refrigerator, where the temperature is between 35° and 50° F. Keep the soil evenly moist while the bulbs are forming roots; check the pots weekly to see if they need water.

At the forcing stage, bring the pots out of the cool environment into warmth and light, which will trigger the formation of leaves and flowers in three to four weeks. The bulbs are ready for forcing when the tips begin to push up through the soil. For a succession of blooms over a long period, begin forcing a few pots each week and place them in a sunny, cool (55° to 70° F) spot. The cooler the area, the longer the flowers will last. Keep the soil moist and keep the bulbs away from radiators and gas heaters; flower buds will fail to open if the soil dries out. Bring all bulbs into a warm and sunny location by late February.

After the flowers fade, keep the foliage in good health by continuing to provide moisture and sunlight. As soon as any danger of heavy frost is past, move the bulbs to an out-of-the-way place outdoors where the foliage can continue to mature and produce food for next year's blooms. Bulbs will not stand forcing for a second year. Some of them, especially tulips, are best discarded after forcing. Daffodils, however, can be transplanted into the garden in spring and will produce a full bloom again in two or three years.

Problems in forcing bulbs are few:

• Tulips almost always show some aphids, either on the leaves when they emerge from the soil or on the flower buds.

• Flower buds of forced bulbs will blast (fail to open) if the soil is allowed to dry out after they've begun to grow.

• Sometimes bulbs succumb to basal rot. If the foliage suddenly turns yellow and stops growing, give it a gentle tug. If the foliage is loose, there's a rootless rotted bulb in the soil. Discard both the bulb and the soil to prevent the disease from spreading.

Forcing Tender Narcissus

Hardy daffodils require a lengthy period of cold temperatures to bloom, but there are also some tender narcissus, such as 'Paper White' and 'Soleil d'Or', which are precooled and can be forced relatively quickly in a somewhat sunny or sunny location. Successive plantings made about two weeks apart from mid-October to December will provide indoor blooms from Thanksgiving to St. Patrick's Day.

Plant the bulbs among moist pebbles, in a light potting mix, or in a homemade mix with equal parts soil, sand, and peat moss. Place the bases of the bulbs at a depth of 1 to 1½ inches in the growing medium; then water thoroughly. Drain and set away in a cool (50° to 65° F), dark place until the roots form. After the bulbs have grown a good root system—which usually takes two to four weeks—bring them into a warm room with bright sunlight. They will quickly send up clusters of white or gold blossoms.

Discard 'Paper White' narcissus after forcing if you live in an area where winter temperatures dip below 20° F. In warmer regions plant them in the garden outdoors. But don't try to force these bulbs again. Buy new stock each year for forcing.

'Paper Whites' (Narcissus) *are popular and easy bulbs to force.*

Forcing Hyacinths and Crocuses in Water

Hyacinths and crocuses are often grown in specially designed containers that hold the bulb above a well of water into which the roots grow. These containers are often made of glass, and growing these bulbs in glass containers is especially fun for children, who can watch the roots and flowers develop.

Fill the container so that the base of the bulb is just above the water, and add water as needed to maintain this level. The bulb should not touch the water or it will rot. Change the water every three or four weeks. A small piece of charcoal in the water will deter harmful bacteria. Place the container in a dark, cool area until roots have formed (about 14 weeks); then move it into the light.

Forcing Flowering Branches

The delicate beauty of flowering branches of cherry, forsythia, pussy willow, and flowering quince and other outdoor trees and shrubs can bring springtime indoors during those cold days of late winter. You can force the blooms on a branch of any of these outdoor plants to use indoors as a flowering decorative accent.

Cut 2- to 3-foot branches during February or March when the flower buds have begun to swell. (If you cut too soon, the flowers will not open.) Smash the cut ends of the branches with a hammer to help the branches absorb water, and then place them in a large container of water in a moderately cool (60° to 70° F), bright room (however, pussy willows that have already opened should not be placed in water). Change the water every few days. In about two weeks, blossoms will appear.

The blossoms will open quickly in a warm room but will last longer in a cool room. Heat and light promote the development of flowers; cool temperatures and darkness retard flower development and help to make the flowers last longer. To prolong the flowering period once it has begun, some gardeners dip the stem ends into wax to seal the cut surface, and others trim the stem ends every day or so. Placing copper pennies in the vase water, dipping the stem ends in fruit preservative, and soaking the stems in warm water and then refrigerating them are also popular practices.

Forcing Annual Flowers

Some of summer's brightest annual flowers force easily in rooms with full sun and a moderately cool (60° to 70° F), humid atmosphere. (Browallia and torenia will make do with less sun—good sunlight from an east window is ample.) In addition to brightening your own home, they make cheerful gifts for friends.

Hyacinths (Hyacinthus orientalis) *are easy bulbs to force. Growing several plants in matching containers allows you to create an impressive arrangement.*

A temperature range of 60° to 70° F is ideal for forcing annuals. Pot the flowers in a mixture of equal parts soil, sand, and peat moss, keeping them evenly moist. Fertilize the plants every two weeks with liquid houseplant food and pinch the growing tips as necessary to encourage compact, bushy plants. Aphids are likely to be troublesome.

To grow ageratum, sweet alyssum, dwarf balsam, browallia, and dwarf cockscomb indoors for winter and early spring bloom, sow seeds in early August. Follow the same technique for dwarf marigolds, sweet peas, nasturtiums, and morning glories. Once the seedlings are large enough to handle, transplant them to individual pots, and continue moving the plants

Flowering branches can be forced into early blossom for an indoor display. The branches can be arranged in a vase or planted in a large container to simulate a living tree.

Summer comes early when its brightest annual flowers are forced into bloom for indoor color. A centerpiece of marigolds, lobelia, ivy, and sweet alyssum echoes the colors found throughout the dining room.

to larger containers as they increase in size, stopping at 5- to 7-inch containers. Provide a trellis for morning glory and sweet pea vines, and try hanging baskets for the trailing plants.

Lobelia, nicotiana, petunia, snapdragon, torenia, and verbena can be dug from outdoor plantings in autumn, before the first frost, and carefully potted in 5- to 10-inch containers. Disturb roots as little as possible, but cut back leaves and stems severely to encourage new growth. Keep plants in a cool, shady place for a few days while they get accustomed to the pots. Then place them in a sunny indoor location, such as on a windowsill, and keep them moist.

Forcing Hardy Perennials

Forcing hardy perennials is a specialized gardening technique that few people even try. However, if you have an outdoor perennial border that abounds with hosta, bleeding-heart, astilbe, or lily-of-the-valley, you may want to try forcing them in winter.

Dig vigorous clumps in early fall, trim them back, and pot them in a moist mixture of soil, sand, and peat moss. Place them in a cold frame, an unheated garage, or a cool attic, away from the danger of a severe frost. In midwinter, bring the pots indoors to a moderately cool (60° to 65° F), sunny windowsill. Keep the soil evenly moist. When new leaves begin to grow, fertilize them every two weeks with a houseplant fertilizer. With luck, some of spring's loveliest flowers will appear weeks or months before their outdoor counterparts.

After forcing hardy perennials, replant them outdoors. Do not force the same clumps again for at least two years.

EXTENDING THE FLOWERING SEASON OF OUTDOOR PLANTS

Many tender perennial flowers grown outdoors in warm weather as annuals can be brought inside before a frost for an extended flowering

This pink astilbe, a perennial normally found outdoors, was forced to bloom indoors in time for Easter.

season. They will, however, require a sunny indoor location and moist air. On a sunny windowsill, under fluorescent lights, or in a home greenhouse, some plants will bloom indefinitely. Others will merely yield a few more flowers before they die.

Plants can be dug out of the garden and potted, although they will suffer more shock than a potted plant that is simply transferred indoors. The best time to dig up and pot a plant is two to three weeks before the first frost date.

Water the plant a day or two before you plan to dig it up. This will make your work easier and help protect the plant from root damage. Using either a sturdy trowel or a spade, dig up the plant with a sizable chunk of earth surrounding the root system and follow the potting instructions on page 55.

Leave the newly potted plant outdoors in a shady, moist spot for several days so that it can acclimatize to the container and the lower light. Scrutinize for pests and diseases and groom the plant as carefully as you would indoor plants that have vacationed outside (see pages 60 to 62).

Annual or tender perennial flowers that send up sturdy new basal growth whenever their tops are cut back are the best to save as houseplants. These include wax begonias (*Begonia* × *semperflorens-cultorum*), geraniums, and impatiens.

Once these plants are indoors, keep them moist. After they have adjusted and begun to grow again, feed them monthly with a liquid fertilizer and clip off spent blooms. These plants are ideal for temporarily filling a new greenhouse.

You can bring in frost-sensitive bulbous plants, such as caladium, achimenes, tuberous begonia, and amaryllis. The less hardy herbs, such as borage, lemon verbena, sweet basil, marjoram, young parsley, scented geraniums, and in cold climates, sweet bay and rosemary, can also be potted and brought indoors.

A row of red-leaved caladium lines the window at the end of a hall. Below, calathea fills the space next to the chair. These tender perennials, favorites in outdoor gardens, also make excellent indoor plants.

Greenhouses and Solariums

In the controlled environment of a greenhouse or solarium, flowers bloom all winter, and plants that often struggle to survive outside grow easily to their full potential.

Entering a greenhouse for the first time is like stepping into another world. It may be snowing outside, but inside a greenhouse you are transported to the steamy, languid tropics or springtime in the desert, surrounded by exotic orchids or lush displays of succulents. Greenhouses and solariums let you create an ideal environment for your plants. They also work well as growing stations, providing you with a year-round supply of houseplants for display stations throughout your home.

Today's greenhouses and solariums are simple, practical, and no longer exclusively the domain of the wealthy. They can be freestanding structures, add-ons to the house, or window extensions over a kitchen sink or in a corner of a living room. A greenhouse fits wherever you have space: in a window, on a balcony, in the background, or on the roof.

This chapter discusses the many types of greenhouses and solariums, their best uses, and some basics on caring for plants in these settings.

The protected environment of a greenhouse is ideal for year-round gardening.

GREENHOUSES

The term *greenhouse* refers to any structure that traps and stores the sun's energy by means of transparent panels. In common parlance, however, a greenhouse is a structure specifically designed to have as much transparent surface as possible oriented toward the sun. A sun porch, a sunroom, or even a sunny window can function as a greenhouse.

Freestanding Greenhouses

Greenhouses are usually either lean-tos or freestanding. Freestanding greenhouses, by far the more common type and what most people mean when they mention greenhouses, are especially popular among serious hobbyists. Such hobbyists use the greenhouse as a general working area, devoting space to aisles, shelves, rows of hanging plants, and a workbench for potting, propagating, and caring for their plants. The layout of the interior space is usually entirely practical, with easy access for a loaded wheelbarrow through doors at either end.

Freestanding greenhouses can be built to any size and covered with glass, acrylic, or fiberglass. The smaller greenhouses that are becoming increasingly available are appropriate for most gardeners. They allow you to add to your outdoor growing season by intensifying the warmth and humidity of a section of a backyard or balcony without going to the trouble of installing a foundation, plumbing, and lights.

Solariums and Greenhouse Rooms

Solariums, or sunrooms, have become important architectural elements in many modern homes. Builders and remodelers install them because of their unique appeal as an indoor-outdoor living space and because of the benefits of adding sun-provided warmth and light to the space. Although these additions are often not primarily designed for indoor gardeners, they are as effective as a greenhouse for plants that enjoy plenty of direct light.

A solarium is an ideal spot for sun lovers—plants and people—yet both can be fried if there are no blinds or screens to control the intensity of the light. Even with screens, a south-facing solarium will be much warmer than other rooms in the home.

Greenhouse Additions

The latest trend in indoor growing space is the greenhouse addition. Unlike the spacious solarium, which is designed primarily for lounging and relaxation and only secondarily for plants, the greenhouse addition is a space devoted to

Two freestanding greenhouses allow this hobbyist to specialize in plants that require different growing conditions.

Top: Indoors and outdoors appear to meld into one enchanting space in this dramatic solarium.
Bottom: This sunroom is ideal for plants and is also a pleasant setting for conversation or reading.

plants. It is usually smaller and more intimate than a solarium and seen not so much as a room of its own but as an extension of the one to which it is attached. A greenhouse addition opens up a room to the outdoors.

The kitchen is a perfect room for a greenhouse addition; you can grow herbs and vegetables just where you need them and harvest them without having to deal with the variable conditions of the great outdoors. Greenhouse additions are also just the place for producing attractive flowering plants to decorate less sunny areas of the house while they are in flower.

Greenhouse additions can be custom built to suit the style of the home; more often, though, they are installed from kits either by the homeowner or by a professional crew. Usually the expense of a new foundation is eliminated by using an existing patio or balcony as a base and the costs for new heating, water, and electric services are avoided by simply extending those from the house. A greenhouse addition is particularly effective in an urban home: It takes up little outdoor space yet greatly increases the feeling of space indoors.

Greenhouse Windows

If the idea of a greenhouse interests you, a full-sized one is not the only option and may not be the right one. It can be costly to install and

A south-facing greenhouse window in a sunny kitchen is the ideal spot for a prized collection of cacti and succulents.

Access to a nearby faucet will make watering easier, which makes bathroom windows a good choice, doubly so in the case of a kitchen window, as you would be able to grow fresh herbs and vegetables within arm's reach. Choose a window that has a view that you won't miss, since a plant-filled greenhouse window does not allow a clear outlook from the inside of the house. This can be a distinct advantage. Consider using a window greenhouse to divert attention from an uninteresting vista, such as the wall of a neighboring apartment building.

Once you've found the right window, choose a kit to fit it. First measure the window carefully. The easiest window greenhouses to install are those that fit directly onto the outside window frame. Kits are available to suit all standard frame sizes. If you can't find a kit that fits your window exactly, buy one that is slightly larger and install a new frame around the old frame.

Glass structures are the most popular because they allow a clear view outdoors, but they are expensive and also heavy, making installation more difficult. Double-wall acrylic structures are just as durable and are far lighter, making them the next best choice. Choose a structure that suits the style of your house: There is often a choice of frames, including ones made of wood, aluminum, or PVC (polyvinyl chloride, a type of plastic).

The best window greenhouses come with temperature-controlled vents that open automatically to let out hot air. However, even with these greenhouses, it is wise to install a small circulating fan near the window to blow warm air into the structure in winter and vent hot air in summer. Because of their small size, window greenhouses tend to heat up quickly during the day and cool off rapidly at night.

There is an extremely simple alternative to even the window greenhouse. You can purchase a miniature indoor greenhouse and place it on a windowsill or on a shelf under lights. Miniature greenhouses have many uses: propagating new plants, curing ailing plants that have been suffering from insufficient humidity, isolating sick plants during treatment, and forcing flowering plants into bloom. They can also make attractive permanent homes for humidity-loving tropical species. Altogether, they are a useful addition to the indoor garden.

operate and may take up too much space on an urban lot. A greenhouse window, however, is well within most budgets, and just about everyone has at least one window to work with.

Greenhouse windows do not require expensive plumbing, electricity, or heating systems: The systems in the house or apartment will be adequate. Kits can be assembled in as little as one afternoon. And if the greenhouse window becomes too small for your needs, you can always add another greenhouse window or a full-sized greenhouse later.

Start by choosing an appropriate window. Apply the same criterion as you would when choosing a site for a full-sized greenhouse: the most light possible with the least obstruction. A spot facing full south is best, although one facing east or west is acceptable. Even a north window is suitable as long as you install fluorescent lights. An overhanging roof is not always a major hindrance and can even be an advantage; it will reduce heat buildup and excessive light in summer when the sun is directly overhead yet allow the light to flood in, unobstructed, in winter, when the sun is lower on the horizon.

GREENHOUSE USES

A greenhouse can be put to any number of uses besides growing a range of ornamentals. The most frequent uses are for decoration of the home, solar heating, plant collections, and food production.

Home Decoration

In a greenhouse plants can be grown to a degree of perfection not easy to achieve in the house itself. It is natural to want to show them off to best advantage by bringing them inside, but keep their stays in the house fairly limited or they will lose their greenhouse luster.

Solar Heating

A greenhouse attached to the home is a natural source of passive solar heating. To make the most use of this heating, install a fan or other type of air circulator to force the heated air from the greenhouse into the house. Although there is not likely to be a significant amount of warmth before the first of March or after the middle of October, it can be ample and welcome in March, April, and May.

Plant Collections

A greenhouse is a perfect place to bring similar kinds of plants together in a collection—plants in the same family or genus, plants with the same cultural requirements, or plants that

Top: As long as the sun is out, a greenhouse will trap an amazing amount of heat even on cold winter days. Bottom: Orchids, such as these moth-orchids (Phalaenopsis), *can be easily grown in a greenhouse and then brought indoors to enjoy while they are in bloom.*

Many fruits and vegetables, including exotic crops that are not readily available in supermarkets, grow well in a greenhouse.

Greenhouses are ideal locations for hobbyists to indulge in their favorite specimens. Here, tuberous begonias (Begonia ✕ tuberhybrida) show off their colors.

have the same aesthetic impact. The most common of such groupings are alpines, begonias, bromeliads, gesneriads, orchids, cacti, and succulents.

Alpines prefer a cold, bright environment and are particularly suitable for a solar-heated greenhouse. Begonias and gesneriads share a need for both warmth and shade from the summer sun. Epiphytic bromeliads and orchids, the type grown by most fanciers, require a fibrous, free-draining growing medium. Bromeliad and orchid species run the gamut of temperature tolerance: Some will tolerate near-freezing temperatures; others need a minimum temperature of 50° F or above. Bromeliads prefer a good deal more summer sunlight than do most orchids.

Of all these groups, succulents are best suited to a greenhouse. They accept the extremes of temperature day and night, summer and winter; are unaffected by the sometimes extremely low humidity; and are able to withstand a fair measure of neglect.

Food Production

The environment of a greenhouse is in many ways well suited to food production. Though growing food in a greenhouse is not cost-effective at the outset, using a greenhouse for food production does have benefits: absolute freshness, freedom from contaminants, and the possibility of growing exotic varieties that are unavailable in local markets.

Vegetables, fruits, and herbs can all be successfully grown in a greenhouse. Off-season vegetable crops are particularly popular, especially in cold-winter areas.

GROWING PLANTS IN A GREENHOUSE

Since a greenhouse is a controlled environment, there's no trick to growing pineapples or papayas in Montana or Maine. Just choose the exotic fruits you want for Thanksgiving dinner or the flowers for your anniversary centerpiece and follow the care requirements. The real fun is in working with nature. Once you understand the natural cycle of a plant, you will learn to care for it according to its needs. In return, it will give you pleasure, nourishment, and beauty.

The needs of houseplants in a greenhouse are much the same as of those kept in the home. Most successful commercial plant nurseries use the same growing media for greenhouse container plants as they do for other indoor plants. Watering requirements are also much the same as for houseplants indoors. Remember to water according to the needs of the plant rather than by the clock or calendar.

Whenever any plant is watered, some nutrients leach out of the soil and need to be replaced with a fertilizer. The amount of fertilizer required at any one time is extremely small, but the need is continuous. Mixing a timed-release fertilizer into the soil while you are potting a plant is the easiest way to ensure continual fertilization.

Bottom Heat

One thing you can do in any sort of greenhouse that you can't do in a home is heat the growing medium to a controlled temperature. This produces often dramatically healthier and more vigorous plants.

Heating the growing medium has several beneficial effects on the plants. In heated soil most tropical and subtropical plants can tolerate cooler air temperatures than normal; so plants usually grown in hot, humid greenhouses may thrive in a greenhouse that is cooler and drier. Moisture-laden air that escapes from the soil raises the humidity around the plants, a condition favored by tropical and subtropical species. Bottom heat also stimulates root growth and increases a plant's resistance to disease, which in turn stimulates more foliage growth. In addition, many tropical plants will bloom all year in heated soil.

The merits of providing bottom heat are well known, but the cost of heating the soil has prevented it from becoming a common practice in commercial greenhouses. In small greenhouses or indoor planters, where energy requirements are much lower, it may barely increase the monthly utility bill. In a greenhouse the air can be kept almost 20° F cooler if the soil is heated. This saves on heating costs and brings the temperature and humidity into a range closer to that of indoor living spaces, making the air in the greenhouse more comfortable for you and easing the transition of plants from the greenhouse to display stations throughout your home.

For optimum growth and flowering, heat the growing medium to around 70° F. Fluctuations below 70° F are acceptable, since these occur in native habitats. However, temperatures over 85° F are undesirable; the soil dries out quickly and small roots will die.

Check the temperature with a thermometer. To avoid breaking the thermometer, dig a hole and gently place the thermometer in it; then cover the bulb of the thermometer with the growing medium.

Many plants respond well to bottom heat. Tropical palms, for instance, generally respond with prodigious root growth. Repot the palm as soon as new roots come through the drainage hole. Many tropical species of the Acanthus family produce more flowers when grown in warm soil. Among these are the lollipop-plant (*Pachystachys lutea*), a medium shrub with bright yellow bracts and unusual white flowers, and king's-crown (*Justicia carnea*), a shrub with fist-sized clusters of pink flowers.

All the thunbergia vines do well in heated soil. So do the monkey-plants (*Ruellia*), including *R. makoyana*, which has large, rose-red, trumpet-shaped flowers, and *R. graecizans*, which has orange-red bracts and flowers. Many

Bottom heating the soil with electric coils often produces healthier and more vigorous plants.

tropical bulbs and tuberous plants also thrive with bottom heat. The spectacular glory lilies (*Gloriosa rothschildiana*), caladiums, achimenes, and florist's gloxinias (*Sinningia speciosa*) are in this group. Indoor vegetable gardeners may want to try bottom heat for tomatoes, peppers (both bell and hot varieties), eggplant, chayote, tropical vegetable varieties, and cultivated mushroom species.

There are a number of ways of providing bottom heat to the growing medium. You can do it by applying heat directly. You can also apply heat indirectly to the pot or bench that is in contact with the soil.

Electric cables heat the growing medium directly. Small cables work well in containers, window boxes, and propagation benches. They are simple to install and operate. Use the highest-quality cables you can afford, since cheaper ones may crack or deteriorate in damp soil and require frequent replacement. Electric cables are useful for starting seeds, growing plants from cuttings or seedlings, and establishing large specimen plants during their first year or two after transplanting.

Cables are available in a variety of forms, with and without built-in thermostats. Probably the most convenient is a propagation mat, which resembles an electric heating pad. A propagation mat heats the area it covers.

If you are not buying a mat, the length of cable you need depends on the area you are heating and on the capacity of the particular brand of cable. As a general rule of thumb, use 2 to 4 linear feet of cable, or 10 to 15 watts, per square foot.

Lay the cable on the bottom of the plant container, being careful not to overlap the strands (clothespins are useful tools for holding the cable in place). Cover the cable with about an inch of sand. Place pieces of screen on top of the sand, to avoid damaging the cable with tools. The growing medium then is placed on top of the screen.

Another method for heating the growing medium relies on hot water from a gas or electric hot-water heater or from a solar collector. In these systems the hot water circulates through plastic pipes and neoprene tubing. For a hobby greenhouse ½-inch plastic pipe and ⅛-inch neoprene tubing are adequate. Kits are available, complete with special fittings to attach the tubing to the pipe.

A gardener who grows many different plants in different-sized containers may prefer a simpler system. For small greenhouses you can easily make a soil-heating system by casting a concrete slab bench. Simply place plastic or copper tubing in the form, pour the concrete, hook up the connections, and place your potted plants or flats on the heated bench. This kind of bench is easy to clean, and it radiates heat throughout the greenhouse as well as heating the pots directly on top of it.

Many of the supplies needed for a soil-heating system are available at hardware and plumbing stores. Stores selling solar heating supplies are good sources for tubing and valves. Small soil-heating cables are available at many garden stores.

Pots or Not?

There are two general ways to grow plants in a greenhouse: in containers or directly in the ground. For greenhouses that form a part of the living space, pots will be the first choice. In freestanding greenhouses, the choice depends on the goals of the gardener and the requirements of the plants.

Plants in the ground   Growing plants in the ground allows you to make an integrated garden

Top: The owner of this greenhouse has created an impressive desert scene, having set plants directly into the ground.
Bottom: Countless plant species from around the world can be displayed in a greenhouse setting. Light and temperature are controlled by opening the panels and the door. Cacti grow on the warmer and lighter upper shelves, orchids below.

design. You can grow plants close enough to-gether so that they enhance one another through flower color, foliage pattern, or shape.

Growing plants in the ground is also easier. Plants growing in the ground require much less frequent watering than plants in pots, and they are much less vulnerable to stress if watering is delayed. Problems with drainage, feeding, and salt buildup are also less likely.

In general, plants in the ground are healthier and therefore better looking and more resistant to pests and cold. They also grow more vigorously, which may be desirable.

Plants in pots   Plants in pots can be easily moved around the greenhouse or in and out of it. They are easier to display indoors at flowering time or to move outdoors for a rest. It is not a good idea to grow plants in pots in a greenhouse where temperatures fall below freezing because their roots are particularly vulnerable to frost damage.

DISPLAYING PLANTS IN GREENHOUSES AND SOLARIUMS

Plants in attached greenhouses, solariums, and greenhouse windows should contribute to the overall design of the room. Display stations should suit the cultural needs of the plant and the design needs of the room.

Display plants in freestanding greenhouses to suit both you and the plant. Ideally, benches and cabinets inside a greenhouse are both functional and attractive. They should fit your own needs, taking your height and reach into consideration so that you can tend your plants comfortably. Many manufactured benches have casters so they will roll back and forth. These benches greatly increase the usable growing area in a greenhouse.

Other popular bench styles include stair-step benches and planter benches. Stair-step benches give you more display room. Shade-loving plants can go under the bench. On any bench you will need to rotate the plants regularly unless they are located against a white wall; otherwise, they will grow unevenly toward the sun.

Planter benches can be filled with soil, but be careful to prevent the plants from becoming waterlogged. Some gardeners fill planter benches with soaked vermiculite and place potted plants on top of them. This way the plants will remain well watered for days.

Whichever benches you choose, they should provide a good display area for the plants and have maximum light exposure. They should allow air to circulate freely through them and among the plants. Use an open-grid material, such as expanded metal or snow fencing, for the bench surface.

Plants growing in pots have the advantage of being portable. They can be rearranged into varying displays at different seasons or as the gardener's mood dictates.

U.S. Measure and Metric Measure Conversion Chart

		Formulas for Exact Measures				Rounded Measures for Quick Reference		
	Symbol	When you know:	Multiply by:	To find:				
Mass	oz	ounces	28.35	grams		1 oz		= 30 g
(Weight)	lb	pounds	0.45	kilograms		4 oz		= 115 g
	g	grams	0.035	ounces		8 oz		= 225 g
	kg	kilograms	2.2	pounds		16 oz	= 1 lb	= 450 g
						32 oz	= 2 lb	= 900 g
						36 oz	= 2¼ lb	= 1000 g (1 kg)
Volume	pt	pints	0.47	liters		1 c	= 8 oz	= 250 ml
	qt	quarts	0.95	liters		2 c (1 pt)	= 16 oz	= 500 ml
	gal	gallons	3.785	liters		4 c (1 qt)	= 32 oz	= 1 liter
	ml	milliliters	0.034	fluid ounces		4 qt (1 gal)	= 128 oz	= 3¾ liter
Length	in.	inches	2.54	centimeters		⅜ in.	= 1 cm	
	ft	feet	30.48	centimeters		1 in.	= 2.5 cm	
	yd	yards	0.9144	meters		2 in.	= 5 cm	
	mi	miles	1.609	kilometers		2½ in.	= 6.5 cm	
	km	kilometers	0.621	miles		12 in. (1 ft)	= 30 cm	
	m	meters	1.094	yards		1 yd	= 90 cm	
	cm	centimeters	0.39	inches		100 ft	= 30 m	
						1 mi	= 1.6 km	
Temperature	°F	Fahrenheit	⅝ (after subtracting 32)	Celsius		32° F	= 0° C	
	°C	Celsius	⅝ (then add 32)	Fahrenheit		212° F	= 100° C	
Area	in.²	square inches	6.452	square centimeters		1 in.²	= 6.5 cm²	
	ft²	square feet	929.0	square centimeters		1 ft²	= 930 cm²	
	yd²	square yards	8361.0	square centimeters		1 yd²	= 8360 cm²	
	a.	acres	0.4047	hectares		1 a.	= 4050 m²	